# The Jazz of Preaching

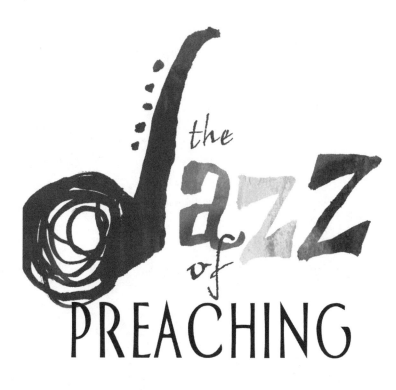

# the Jazz of PREACHING

How to preach with great freedom and joy

Kirk Byron Jones

Abingdon Press
*Nashville*

THE JAZZ OF PREACHING
HOW TO PREACH WITH GREAT FREEDOM AND JOY



*This book is printed on acid-free paper.*

**Library of Congress Cataloging-in-Publication Data**

Jones, Kirk Byron.
The jazz of preaching : how to preach with great freedom and joy / Kirk Byron Jones.
p. cm.
ISBN 0-687-00252-4 (binding: adhesive, pbk. : alk. paper)
1. Preaching. 2. Jazz—Religious aspects—Christianity. I. Title.

BV4211.3.J66 2004
251—dc22

2004003045



04 05 06 07 08 09 10 11 12 13 — 10 9 8 7 6 5 4 3 2 1

MANUFACTURED IN THE UNITED STATES OF AMERICA

*To the Jazz Spirit*

*To Ella, Louie, Duke, and Jimmy Scott*

*To My Students in the Jazz of Preaching Classes at Andover Newton Theological School*

*There is, of course, no way of recreating the atmosphere—the fervor of the congregation, the amens and hallelujahs, the undertone of singing which was often a soft accompaniment to parts of the sermon; nor the personality of the preacher—his [her] physical magnetism, his [her] gestures and gesticulations, his [her] changes of tempo, his [her] pauses for effect, and more than all, his [her] tones of voice.*

—James Weldon Johnson,
from the preface to
*God's Trombones*

# Contents

CHAPTER ONE

# Let There Be Jazz

*Jazz is about finding and sharing who you are.*
—Betty Carter

*What surprises there are! We are such planners! We decide how God must come into human affairs. We treat it all with a kind of public relations twist. We pick the time and the place. We insure that the right people are there to meet God. We get the news releases out as to what to expect. We even have some prepared quotes. But God has an uncanny way of taking care of times and places and entrances. While we wait at the airport, as it were, with a representative committee of dignitaries, an escort waiting for the coming, God has a way of quietly arriving at the bus station, walking up the side street, and slipping, unnoticed, through the servant's chambers.*
—Gene Bartlett

## Songs in the Night

It was Saturday night, and I didn't have a clue about what to preach the next day. My situation worsened when I realized that I didn't have it in me to get up a sermon, to at least start one that I could develop and polish a little in the morning. I had been in this place before. Having been a "boy preacher," by this time, I had been preaching for over twenty years. This was not my first time being on "E" (for empty) on a Saturday night. But that night the emptiness was deeper than usual. In that moment, my calling was to get as far as possible from sermon preparation and "the call" to preach itself. I needed a ministry respite, a preaching reprieve. One of the greatest preachers of our time, or any time, once confided to me that there were times during his long ministry when the last thing he felt like doing was preaching. He said that in those moments a job as a sanitation worker seemed more appealing.

I was in as deep a preaching slump as I had ever been in. I found myself turning to music, but not the inspirational, soothing sounds of gospel music. Instead, perhaps as an act of defiance, I placed a jazz CD in the disc player, *The Intimate Ella*, and began listening to Ella Fitzgerald, accompanied by pianist Paul Smith. I do not recall searching for the disk, or wanting to hear Ella Fitzgerald in particular. I knew she was a noteworthy performer, but that's all I knew. I didn't know that I was listening to a singer commonly referred to as "The First Lady of Song." I had no idea that she was once defined by Duke Ellington as being "beyond category."

If you are a jazz enthusiast or a fan of Ella Fitzgerald, you can probably guess what happened next. As Ella Fitzgerald sang, something happened that was totally unexpected; I began to cry. Her angelic voice was simultaneously soft and piercing. Her singing, soulfully caressed the lyrics of songs like "I Cried for You," "My Melancholy Baby," and "Reach for Tomorrow" melted my misery. This was wonderful and scary at the same time. I had been revived before, but the mode was either gospel music, prayer, or inspirational reading. I had never been delivered by a jazz singer before. An hour later, I felt revived inside. I began preparing the sermon with fresh energy, and the next day I ministered with new strength and joy. No joke. Or, holy joke of the highest order.

In *Listen to Your Life,* Frederick Buechner writes, "Whenever you find tears in your eyes, especially unexpected ears, it is well to pay close attention."[1]

I became deeply curious about what had happened that Saturday evening. How and why did this person's singing move me so? How could something "worldly" like jazz music wield such spiritual power? Does all jazz music contain such potency?

The seed for *The Jazz of Preaching* was planted that Saturday night, or maybe many years earlier. Believe it or not, I was born and reared in New Orleans, the birthplace of jazz. Looking back on it all now: New Orleans, preaching, Saturday night blues, Ella, I think I was caught in a sacred setup. In fact, one of my youthful talents was doing a singing impression of Louis Armstrong. But apart from this minimal musical antic, I don't recall any other connection to jazz while growing up in New Orleans. Perhaps this would have been different had I not concluded my drum playing at the end of sixth grade. My jazz roots meant nothing to me until Ella sang to me. I once heard jazz great, and fellow New Orleanean, Wynton Marsalis, say during an awards show, "When you are ready to listen, the music is there to be heard." Unbeknown to me my melancholy mood had placed me in listening mode.

I began purchasing jazz music, mostly classic jazz. The music facilitated my entrance into another world inhabited by assorted musical mages. I began developing favorites, including Louis Armstrong, Mary Lou Williams, Duke Ellington, Sarah Vaughan, John Coltrane, Oscar Peterson, Billie Holiday, Lester Young, and an unsung sparrow by the name of Jimmy Scott. I became enthralled with their sounds and their stories. Along the way, I learned more about the history and hallmarks of jazz. I became especially interested in certain features of jazz (creativity, improvisation, dialogue, and more) that were common to various styles of jazz, (big band, bebop, free, and more). After about a year, two rivers began to converge. The river of preaching, one of my first passions in life, and the river of jazz, my newest passion. I began to sense that jazz had a good deal more to offer homiletics than a singular uplift to a lone preacher. What if preachers were as contagiously joyful in their preaching as Louis Armstrong was in his playing and singing? As rich in their sermonic renderings as Sarah Vaughan was in her musical vocals? As honest about heartache as Billie Holiday was every time she sang about the blues of life? As alluringly clear as the angelic voice of Ella Fitzgerald? As patient in pacing as the holy, hesitant singing manner of Jimmy Scott? As tenaciously uninhibited in the action of creating as Duke Ellington?

I sat with my curiosities for another year, and then our esteemed preaching professor at Andover Newton Theological School, Eddie O'Neal, announced his retirement after thirty plus years of service. I had been one of his students. Later, as his faculty colleague, I taught social ethics at Andover Newton for several years while pastoring Ebenezer Baptist Church in Boston. My intention was to keep *preaching* in Boston and *teaching* ethics at Andover Newton. Though I had been preaching for many years and had earned a Doctor of Ministry in preaching from Candler School of Theology, Emory University, I was reluctant to teach preaching. It was almost as if I felt that I could not handle the holiness of preaching in a classroom context. It was too much to hold; it was too big for me. Talk about preaching with tenured preaching practitioners or aspiring preachers in informal settings, yes. Teach preaching in a formal academic setting, no. Perhaps I had been overinfluenced by Howard Thurman's humbling declaration in *With Head and Heart*: "I don't think homiletics can be taught." (If one is going to be overinfluenced by anyone, it may as well be Howard Thurman.)

My homiletical reluctance was sabotaged when my preaching mentor, Dr. O'Neal, looked at me during a meeting in which we discussed several persons and classes that would attempt to fill the wide void of his leaving and said, "You do it; you teach a class." Dr. O'Neal's commissioning and the jazz/preaching curiosities and questions rolling around in my head led to a Jazz of Preaching class at Andover Newton. To my knowledge it was the first such class ever, anywhere. Three cheers for Ella!

Over the past four years, during the most enjoyable teaching/learning experiences of my life, my fabulously open and engaging students and I have made this discovery: *Preaching may be enhanced by exploring key elements of jazz and learning to apply those elements to the act of preaching*. This book is a summary and offering of what we asked, discovered, and taught each other in *The Jazz of Preaching*.

## The Jazz of Preaching Journey

The format for the book is based on my class syllabus which has evolved over the past four years. We will cover themes in the order they are presented in my latest syllabus. Risking the limitation of carefully crafted definition, we will begin with definitions. What do we mean by *jazz* and *preaching*? In chapter 2, you may be amazed to discover how much these two realities have in common in terms of fundamental definition. Their most striking shared meaning is that you can use word after word attempting to define them exactly and still be left holding an insufficient definition. When it comes to defining each, both realities remind me of cotton candy: sweet and vanishing. Neither preaching nor jazz can be explained completely. I suspect (and hope) that no one will ever tender a final and conclusive word about them. That having been said, confession will not mute curiosity; we will strain to hear as much as we can hear and say as much as we can say about jazz and preaching, and their sacred intersection.

Chapter 3, "Dreaming a Song, Hearing a Sermon," takes its title from a fascinating clip in Ken Burns's stellar, if necessarily incomplete, documentary, *Jazz*.[2] Duke Ellington is seen softly touching keys on a piano. An interviewer refers to Ellington's "playing the piano." Ellington, appearing slightly surprised, patiently explains that he is not playing, he is "dreaming." As his fingers touch the keys once again, he reiterates, "That's dreaming." We will savor Ellington's interpretation of the seminal stage of the creative process, and bring it into conversation with Thomas Troeger's understanding of "imagining a sermon." I believe that many contemporary sermons are sabotaged from the start by fast-food imagining and instant dreaming. We usually don't allow nearly enough time for sermon seeding and spreading, for idea forming and framing, for listening, listening, thinking, and listening.

Chapter 4, "A Call to Create," discusses the area of my greatest envy of jazz artists. The best jazz artists possess what Albert Murray refers to as "an experimental disposition." For example, pianist Marc Copland once described his approach to playing as follows: "[My] aesthetic involves making every note count and striving to play notes that I have not played before."[3] I am jolted by these words; I am convicted by them. It is so easy to preach the same themes the same old ways. As a guest preacher in churches and conferences around the county, it is so tempting to rely on road tested stories and sermons. This sort of sermonic sameness may be less deadening to a congregation hearing a sermon for the first time. I can tell you from experience that it is more deadening to the preacher who becomes addicted to the overly favored preaching notes. This chapter is about developing a new-note-disposition, an attitude that smiles on difference and novelty and frowns or is at least suspicious of sameness.

For the jazz artist, sampling and shifting sounds is the point, and there is a sense of expectancy about it all. How can preachers be more freely experimental and more joyfully expectant in preaching? Leaning into preaching as a creative dynamic enterprise can help dampen, or better yet, drench, preaching dryness and dullness. I am convinced that the key to becoming a more creative preacher is becoming a more creative person. As we become persons used to stepping and stretching out of preconceived ways of seeing, we will be more apt to avoid preaching ruts. The challenge is to cultivate a desert thirst for new insights and vision not just for preaching, but for living. If we are creative in life, creativity is more likely to break out in the study and the pulpit.

In chapter 5, we turn our attention to what is for many the definitive hallmark of jazz, improvisation: creating music on the spot. A legendary saxophonist says that he "empties himself" just before each performance. I have heard preachers pray just before preaching, "God, I come to you as an empty pitcher before a full fountain." The same sacred impulse is operative for the saxophonist and the sermonizer. They both understand that all prior preparation must be subjugated because the moment of preaching or playing will demand more than prior preparation. It will demand school-crossing guard alertness to the moment, the crowd, the coparticipants, the mood, the spirit, and the new understandings and combinations of understandings that arrive to a presentation already in flight. Improvisation is attending to all these manifold influences, including prior preparation, during performance. Hearing and feeling these influences and then forging them into some communicative offering is improvisation.

We will discuss formidable barriers to such preaching flexibility and freedom, including self-consciousness and the fear of failure. Finally, I will propose methods for making preaching more improvisational, more open and accepting of life and spirit while preaching.

Rivaling improvisation as the definitive feature of jazz is dialogue, the ability of jazz musicians to play in sync together. Jazz groups, whether they are duos, trios, quartets, sextets, or big bands, must know how to listen as well as play. Through listening a musician knows what notes to play and how to play them, when to rest, and when to enter into the sounding forth again. One must listen well in order to enter well. And when he or she sounds forth, they do so knowing that the contribution is not in vain. Their offering will influence the offerings in waiting. Musicians influence each other in regard to sound and spirit. In much of jazz, musicians call and respond to each other, sometimes overtly and directly, sometimes covertly and more intuitively.

There are dialogical dimensions to preaching. Effective preaching depends on how good a speaker and listener you are. Preaching involves multiple dialogical partners including God, congregation, the text, the sermon, current events, the setting, the mode, intrusions, surprises, pauses, deletions, additions, and, yes, the preacher. The ever growing, never-ever-having-arrived preacher is always developing a widening capacity to be engaged in conversation with these partners, sometimes simultaneously.

Less daunting than it sounds, it is a matter of entering the music and dance of dialogue not just for sermon's sake but for life's sake. As is the case with creativity, our dialogical skills for preaching are greatly enhanced by exercising our dialogical muscles in the natural ebb and flow of everyday life.

I must tell you a story that can't wait for the body of the text. I once asked the late Cynthia Perry Ray, wife of the late Reverend Sandy F. Ray, what made her husband such a great preacher. She smiled and responded, "Sandy loved people." I nodded but felt that she had misheard my question. What she said sounded like a good answer to the question, "What made your husband a great pastor?" I made small talk for a moment, and decided to launch my question again, "I know your husband was a great pastor, but what made him a great preacher?" She smiled again, even more broadly this time and said, "I told you, my husband loved people." I have never forgotten that exchange. What she said in substance was that her husband's effectiveness in the pulpit began in his heart. Having a heart for all the dialogical elements of preaching inspires great preaching more readily and regularly. More about the dialogue of jazz and preaching in chapter 6.

Chapter 7 is about preaching in the valley of heartache, *blues preaching*. Blues and jazz come from the same root of African American experience. Blues is feeling flung into a sentiment, a sound, a hum, a moan, a song. The essential ingredient of the blues is not sadness, but honesty. The blues song tradition is the moving, magnificent witness that it is possible to be in sorrow's kitchen, endure pain and suffering, and keep on living. This holy honesty is a necessary part of preaching to the hurting, and preaching with and through our own personal pain. We will discuss how preachers can more effectively and soulfully address congregations struggling in grief. For example, in funeral settings, I have heard ministers play to the tender emotions of the congregation through excess volume and sentimentality. Just as objectionable to me are preachers who rush to joy. They start eulogies in heaven, "where the wicked cease from troubling and the weary are at rest." Real eulogies are not afraid to wait even a long while in the graveyard with the grieving. Death and suffering are no less real than life and joy; the valley is not an illusion. Blues preaching is not afraid to hold heartache; it is only after holding it that it walks haltingly onward.

This chapter is about preaching with honesty, weakness, and budding strength when we are the ones experiencing the pain. One of the greatest challenges of preaching is preaching when you are broken or breaking inside. This brokenness can build through the week, or it can arrive ferociously fresh on Sunday morning. Many things can trigger it, family tension at home, criticism from congregants, lingering concerns about the sermon, mounting tasks to be done that take you over the emotional tipping point. Sometimes these and other realities of life may combine to produce an extended period of preaching with a melancholy spirit. I have been to and through this valley on several occasions. When it comes to preaching through times of emotional strain and pain, the question is not how to preach when your heart is not in it. The question is how to preach with a different heart, with a wounded heart. The wounded heart is no less vital and viable than the upbeat heart, the heart that the majority of television evangelists seem to have all the time. The upbeat heart is not the only heart we have; the preacher is challenged to preach with different hearts. Blues preaching, owning the wounded heartedness of preaching, can unleash deep powers and new insights unknown to the cheery heart. This is not an ode to pain, but a salute to the full truth of life. Blues preaching is about engaging the full truth of life, including the backside and downside of life. Calvary was not a hoax.

Chapter 8 is about joy in preaching. The words my wife directed at me remain with me. As I headed toward the front door and the punishment of plodding through an unready sermon, Bunnie said, with lightness of heart and voice, "Enjoy your preaching." Enjoy my preaching! This sermon, this day? Her petition was in stark contrast to my heavy mood. Yet her words seemed to be just the word I needed to hear, just the word that God wanted me to hear.

Why shouldn't we enjoy ourselves? After all, we are preaching the gospel, the "good news"! If we are not careful and mindful, ministry and preaching can become more drudgery than delight. It is so easy for ministerial and preaching delight to be overrun by the wild stampede of busyness, expectations, and fears.

There is a necessary heaviness about preaching the gospel that has to do with the ultimate nature of our message. We traverse terrain having to do with life and death. But there is another kind of preaching weightiness that has more to do with our inability to freely celebrate the joy of life. Enter jazz! Have you ever attended a jazz funeral? A jazz band leads a slow, prodding procession to the cemetery. People walk or slow-march to a somber rendition of "Just a Closer Walk with Thee." On the way to the graveyard the prevailing sentiment is "the loss of life." Coming back from the cemetery the *gift of life* takes over the band. A trumpet blows as if it is signaling angels in the far reaches of the cosmos, a deliberate, defiant rhythmic drumbeat commences, and mourners turned merrymakers dance, prance, strut down the street to the most joyous music in the universe at the time. It is the most convincing manifestation I know of the psalmist's proclamation, "Weeping may endure for a night but joy comes in the morning." In the joy chapter, we will examine the forces which may inspire or inhibit *sermonic swing*: preaching with deep gladness. If gospel preaching is burdensome, it is, in a phrase of James Earl Massey, "a burdensome joy."

Now for some closing words. Three years of teaching the Jazz of Preaching leads me to the following conclusions:

(1) *You do not have to be a lover of jazz to appreciate or understand this book.* I can remember going through a period of not understanding why everyone could not hear what I was hearing in certain jazz selections. I remember being disappointed when I would point out a certain arresting combination of sounds to my wife, and she responded with mild amusement. My wife, Bunnie, is a gifted vocalist, and a lover of various kinds of music; jazz is not one of them. Several of my forty-five or so Jazz of Preaching students over the past three years (the class is limited to fifteen students a year) did not enroll out of a fondness for jazz. Most of these students did listen and reflect long enough to grasp a connection between the essential elements of jazz and worthy goals in preaching. In this book, I am not trying to win you over to jazz; I do hope to convince you that jazz holds some understandings for communication that no preacher ought to refuse.

(2) *You do not have to be an experienced preacher to follow the discussions in this book.* My students have been pastors who have been in ministry for forty years or more and persons who had not preached their first sermon. You might think that the senior students had more to offer, and that the quality of our time together hinged on their learned assessments, connections, and interpretations. You would be incorrect. The curiosities and questions raised by preaching novices generated fruitful discussions about preaching fundamentals that were indispensable to our common

inquiry. Moreover, our beginning preachers ensured that terms were carefully defined, that we would take no definition for granted. Rather than finding the rehearsal of fundamentals tedious, preaching veterans welcomed the chance to review and question anew. This led to fresh insight and new visions for preaching.

Finally, I conclude each chapter with a section of exercises to help you incorporate elements of jazz into your preaching. Some of the exercises are based on tried and true practices used in my class. Other exercises were conceived during the writing of this book. I hope you take the time to do some if not all the exercises, and in the spirit of jazz develop some practices of your own. You have to practice the jazz of preaching in order to get it. And, I do want you to *get it*!

I have been preaching for over thirty years. Through the years, I have practiced, studied, and pondered preaching with no small passion. I have drawn lavishly from the wells of ministerial books and periodicals in an attempt to be the most effective preacher I could be. I have been blessed by it all. But this, as well, is my honest truth: *I feel that what I have learned from jazz over the past seven years is as important as all my prior learning about preaching*.

Jazz *can* help you to preach with fresh joy and new freedom.

## Notes

1. Frederick Buechner, *Listen to Your Life* (San Francisco: HarperCollins, 1992), 237.

2. This ten-part documentary aired January 2001, the same month that I taught my first Jazz of Preaching class. The serendipity amazed me. As it turned out, the documentary was a tremendous asset to the class, offering students a chance not only to hear but to see great jazz practitioners in their prime. I strongly

encourage you to view the Burns documentary in conjunction with reading this book. At the very least, view tape one after reading the first chapter. It will give you an overview of the beginnings of jazz. I'll point out other Burns highlights worth viewing as we move along.

3. Bill Milkowski, "Hearsay," *JazzTimes* (October 2002), 22.

CHAPTER TWO

# Holy Common Ground

*There is nothing so secular that it cannot be sacred.*
—Madeleine L'Engle, *Walking on Water*

I hope you do not find it too insulting for me to ask you to begin the body of this book by playing a word game. Fill in the blanks of the following five sentences with words from this selection: *music*, *jazz*, *gospel*, or *preaching*. Use just one word for each blank. You may use a word more than once.

1. ________, can you hear it?
2. ________ is a spirit.
3. Perpetual moments of pure creativity, ________ is abandonment within boundaries, the logical undoing of what you think it's supposed to be.
4. ________ is collective storytelling expressing the history and experience of a people.

5. __________ means no category, allowing for continuous progression.

How did you do?

Now, I will attempt to guess your choices.

1. My guess is that you struggled here, realizing that any of the four words fit. If you aren't that much of a music or jazz fan, chances are you opted for the words *gospel* or *preaching*.

2. You struggled here too, didn't you? Even if you are not a music fan, you may have written *music*, aware of music's power to inspire and sooth.

3. Chances are you did not write *preaching* or *gospel*. I do not remember reading such a statement in books on preaching. If you have a small understanding of jazz, you probably wrote jazz here.

4. I will guess that your decision was between *music* and *preaching*.

5. Normally, preaching or gospel is not thought of in these terms. I will say you chose between *music* and *jazz*.

How did I do?

The statement that we have been playing with and considering in pieces is actually a whole commentary found on jazz drummer Terri Lyne Carrington's CD, *Jazz Is a Spirit*:

> Jazz, can you hear it? Jazz is a spirit. Perpetual moments of pure creativity, jazz is abandonment within boundaries, the logical undoing of what you think it's supposed to be. Jazz is collective storytelling expressing the history and experience of a people. Jazz means no category, allowing for continuous progression. Jazz is a spirit. Can you hear it?

Carrington continues by revealing the source of her definition:

> I always felt uncomfortable when asked what jazz is because I never had an answer that felt right in my being. Then one day my good friend Dianne Reeves told me that she heard Abbey Lincoln, when asked the same question, proclaim, "Jazz Is A Spirit." I immediately realized that I agreed and that she had hit the proverbial nail on the head penning this phrase and I have quoted it, giving her props, ever since.

The music of jazz and gospel preaching share some of the same essential ingredients, which include *sound*, *story*, and *transcendence*.

## The Magnificent Matter of Sound

My binoculars were locked on guitarist George Benson at the JVC Newport Jazz Festival in August 2003. He had just come on stage and was playing his first song. Something was not right. The crowd showed no signs of having picked it up, but Benson had. The sound was right as far as the crowd was concerned; Benson wanted it *just* right. He seemed dissatisfied with the sound he was hearing from his guitar. He looked over to two persons offstage. My binoculars spotted them. For several minutes I followed the unspoken largely "facial expression" dialogue between Benson and his technical crew. After a few attempts at modification were nodded off by Benson, finally the entertainer smiled and moved his head up and down. He had found the sound that he was searching for.

Through sounds we communicate and create. For a long time the definitive sign of a new baby's health was not its presence, but its sound, the sound of its cry. Life *sounds* forth. In the movie *Tap*, the sounds of life are revealed as the secret of the late Sonny Washington's amazing tapping originality. Sonny's son, Max, portrayed by tapping legend Gregory Hines, has the same gift. In a marvelous and memorable scene, Hines's character leads a group of people out of a nightclub onto the streets of New York City to teach them the art of *listening* for the dance. First, he hears the sound of car tires moving across a loose sewer lid. Hines notes the rhythm of the sound and creatively taps what he hears. Next, he hears a horn; he joyously adds the horn step. He walks across the street to a night construction crew, leans in with his ears, hears, and then dynamically hoofs the sound of a jackhammer pounding the earth. The scene climaxes with a band playing, and people dancing the night away to the magical, mundane sounds of the city.

Life sounds forth, as does death. Zora Neale Hurston was just thirteen when her mother, Lucy, died. Hurston remembers the sounds, including the screaming silences, of that day:

> Mama was still rasping out the last morsel of her life. I think she was trying to say something, and I think she was trying to speak to me. What was she trying to tell me? What wouldn't I give to know![1]

Sound, so automatically familiar to those who hear, is no ordinary orchestration. In his book *Music, the Brain, and Ecstasy: How Music Captures Our Imagination*, Robert Jourdain describes the complex physiological process of "sound catching" during a musical concert as follows:

> Sound. Glorious sound. Sound of a kind little encountered outside the cavern, each tone a choir in itself, pure and enduring. Patterns ascend to gyrate in midair, then

> fold into themselves and melt away as even grander designs soar. A wall of a hundred sounds hurls toward eager ears, ricocheting about the cavern roof and muffled by 150 tons of flesh below. Joined by thousands of minute reverberations, tones rain down upon the audience from all sides funneling into ears to climb from vibrating air to trembling membrane to oscillating bone to pulsating fluid to surging electrochemical discharges that spurt like fountains toward an expectant brain.[2]

That last word, *brain*, is the hint that the process of receiving and interpreting sound transcends even complex physical mechanics, and has endless possibilities. We all come to sound with different brains. The brain and its tributaries are home to your thoughts and emotions, realities that are in constant formation and re-formation. We will create some of the alterations ourselves through what we decide to think, do, and remember. The sounds hurtling toward our eager ears, as Jourdain puts it, enters a brain that will interpret it one way or another, depending on the countless influences that conspire to make each of us who we are. Thus, simply put, one sound doesn't fit all. When we hear something, a sound has as many possible interpretations as there are persons. The same sound engenders millions of possible hearings because we hear differently. Popular music happens when people agree on a select number of a vast assortment of possible interpretations. Physically, emotionally, and spiritually, no two persons hear sounds the exact same way. This is why music to one may be noise to another.

Sounds are a magnificent matter. Because sound is not just a matter of something we hear but something we consciously and unconsciously interpret, the repertoire of sounds is endless. Why? We are constantly changing. No two people think or interpret alike; no two people hear alike. The expansive glory of sound is its layered multiplicity. Multiple sounds that may be interpreted multiple ways is an endless ocean. Jazz musicians know about the ocean. They accept the ocean. They swim in the ocean.

Jazz is sound-making on purpose. Its reason for being is to make, celebrate, and discover new sounds. Jazz is a rhythmic, syncopated, tonal sounding of life. Its musical richness is apprehending multifarious sound from life, from nature, from the soul. Thelonious Monk, a jazz original, once said, "I hit the piano with my elbow sometimes because of a certain sound I want to hear, certain chords. You can't hit that many notes with your hands."[3]

I hear more of a greater variety of sounds in jazz than almost any other form of musical expression. It is not just about offering more notes, but offering deepening variations of a single note. The commitment of jazz to explore sound is astounding to me, and entertaining. I offer the following testimony in my book *Rest in the Storm: Self-care Strategies for Clergy and Other Caregivers*:

> When I listen to other forms of music, I am carried away by the song's message or sustained rhythm and melody. When I listen to jazz, however, I slow down my listening to more fully appreciate the precipitation of diverse sounds and combinations.[4]

Jazz is primarily a heard reality; preaching is as well. Musicians play notes; preachers play words. Sometimes they even sing them. In his eulogy of Sandy F. Ray, Gardner Taylor said of Ray's preaching: At the height of his pulpit oratory it was hard to tell whether one heard music half-spoken or speech half-sung.[5]

"Tuning" and "whooping" are forms of black folk preaching in which words become notes. Such preaching by those who do it well, with ability and integrity, can slide into the deep places inaccessible to mere spoken words and bring healing of heart and soul. The title of Gerald L. Davis's book about black song preaching styling is memorably apt: *I Got the Word in Me and I Can Sing It, You Know* (University of Pennsylvania Press, 1988).

Good preachers play words well. They know that how a word sounds is as important as what it means, that the sounding of words can work wonders with their meaning. They know that, in the words of Mark Twain, the difference between the right word and the wrong word is the difference between lightning and a lightning bug. That having been said, too many preachers take words for granted. Perhaps because words serve as the common currency of daily communication, we undervalue their power. Familiarity breeds carelessness.

Preaching carelessness manifests itself in the pulpit through wordiness, using many words—sometimes many of the same words to say the same thing over and over again. In her book *When God Is Silent*, Barbara Brown Taylor laments "overly talkative religion."[6] The Jewish sage Abraham Joshua Heschel once warned of the possibility of "losing faith in the reality of words."[7] We preach in a time of what someone has termed "verbal intoxication." Word care and sound sensitivity have never mattered more.

When it comes to preaching carelessness, speed is often the culprit. Our private and public speech has been negatively affected by our cultural addiction to hurry. Sometimes preachers are in such a rush that they fail to give due diligence to the weight of their words. We are in such a hurry that we don't allow time for the listener to savor what has been said. In this way, we unconsciously signal hearers to disregard what they just heard, or almost heard.

Sometimes word/sound carelessness is revealed in imprecision, not so much in using the wrong word but, more often than not, in settling for the almost right word. Novelist Richard Condon, who stutters, revealed once that he had to have six synonyms ready at all times while talking. Having those words available allowed him to make interchangeable shifts when he stuttered. Imprecision happens when we do not have enough alternative sounds within us to make an interchangeable shift to the right word.

When we say words, people hear much more than the words we say. To put it another way, many realities—conscious and unconscious—play into the saying and the hearing of words. When we say a word, people generate understanding by interpreting the sound of the word as well as the voice, facial expression, presence, emotion, resonance, and conviction behind the word. When we say words with integrity, we utter the sounds of our affections and afflictions that travel through words, sighs, growls, you name it. This explains why preachers are sometimes complimented on saying something they do not remember saying. They may have said it in other unconscious ways of sermonic sounding that can be as influential as the words we grant passage from our mouths. When preaching rings hollow, though words have been sounded, the emptiness has to do with deficiency in these other hidden, but no less vital, dimensions of sounding forth.

Because many ministers preach weekly, and work with words in the natural ebb and flow of ministry, it is easy to overestimate verbal ability. I imagine a special seminar working wonders for us on this front. It would not be the standard preaching workshop that you are probably used to attending. The workshop would be co-taught by a poet and a comedian. That's right, a poet and a comedian. No preachers need apply to teach this seminar. I can't think of any other professions that value words more. Poets can teach preachers much about precision, about listening longer in preparation and during the preaching act for the right word or phrase to emerge. Comedians can teach us much about inflection, nuance, and pacing. They know that a great joke can be ruined by poor timing, or saying the right word in the wrong way. Both can teach us about pausing, the unsung essential of effective verbal communication. As there is no music without rests, there is no preaching without pauses. Indeed, as Frederick Buechner reminds us, before the gospel is a word it is silence.[8] Abraham Joshua Heschel observes (standing alongside the poet and comedian) that the strength of faith is in silence, and in words that hibernate and wait.[9]

## Jazz and Preaching: Storytelling Affairs

> *Jazz is collective storytelling expressing the history and experience of a people.*
>
> —Terri Lyne Carrington

Carrington is referring to the story of suffering, soaring Africans and African Americans who created jazz. Jazz is storytelling because its chief musical sources were rooted in the ongoing living narrative of life. Rhythmic and dialogical (instruments and voices calling and responding to each other), African music was an integral part of the natural ebb and flow of everyday life. African music was not ancillary entertainment; it was functional, at the core of everyday life, having to do with work and play, and life and death. Slavery did not destroy this life-rooted rhythm and dialogue; it transformed it, and slaves and former slaves danced and sang with new sounds and steps of oppression and pain.

But they kept on dancing and singing, kept on, in the words of Maya Angelou, "loving life and daring to live it." Slaves and former slaves played, sang, and danced their story, their life experience in places like Congo Square, a grassy plain in northwestern New Orleans, the acknowledged birthplace of jazz, and my hometown.

Such musical expressions, infused with the juices, sensibilities, and longings of everyday life, merged with new, similar "life-ish" musical expressions, notably the spirituals and the blues. African music and black life in a strange land spawned the spirituals and the blues. The spirituals and the blues are stories of black languishing, longing, and hope. As James Cone has said, the spirituals and the blues "flow from the same bedrock of experience."[10]

What you just read between the lines is that jazz was, in part, born in the church. Stories about the first great jazz personality, legendary New Orleans trumpeter Buddy Bolden, bring the unsung, sacred secular kinship to light:

> He is known regularly to have worshipped at the St. John Baptist Church, celebrated for the special fervor with which its congregation sang spirituals and jubilees. The trombonist Kid Ory alleged that Bolden also often attended a Holiness church at Jackson and Franklin "but not for religion, he went there to get ideas on music. He'd hear those songs and he would change them a little. In those . . . churches they sometimes had drums and a piano while the people sang and clapped their hands. Sometimes they'd have guests and invite a trumpet player or a trombone player to come over and play with them. . . . That's where Buddy got it from and that's how it all started."[11]

Jazz music is a gumbo of life music traditions, traditions that sought to truthfully convey the story of life, its hallelujahs and its horrors.

When you listen to jazz, it is possible to hear many stories at the same time. There is the collective history that you may hear, depending on your knowledge of that history. But there are other stories. There is the story of the musical composition itself, the story the composer wants to tell. There is the story of the artist. The element of the artist's story is acknowledged by contemporary jazz singer Lizz Wright:

> A lot of times, I'll just live with a song. I'll listen to it over and over again for months. And all of a sudden, when I sing it or listen to it again, there's something there. It's almost like there's a little basket in my subconscious, and I've been putting things in it.[12]

The story of jazz, collective and personal, is always in formation. Jazz forms and re-forms itself. Usually it is the deliberate intention of the jazz artist to play the old story in new ways, or play a new story in the open space of freedom, the spiritual quintessential element of jazz. This new story is informed by the collective story of triumph and tragedy, the personal story of composition and interpretation, and the artist's own trudging and soaring imaginings. Jazz pianist-composer Cyrus Chestnut speaks of this kind of creative storytelling homiletically:

> I always keep myself open to any last-minute inspiration because I thrive in the realm of spontaneity.... As long as there is a theme, there can always be variations ... whether it's a jazz standard, a pop song or a gospel hymn. I'm like a minister giving his sermon. He will state his theme; he'll improvise variations on that theme; he'll

> take it to a high point, and then he'll make his closing statement. I'm doing the same thing at the piano.[13]

Preaching does not have to be storytelling. Coaches, parents, teachers, and others preach or proclaim in order to persuade without necessarily telling stories. Gospel preaching, the stuff of this book, is storytelling. To preach the gospel is to retell a story that continues to burn with meaning and vitality. It is a story of chaos, creation, loss, liberation, journey, miracle, and homecoming. Frederick Buechner sees within the story the elements of comedy, tragedy, and fairytale, the combination of which renders a healing narrative that is "too good not to be true."

I remember first hearing the story and its constituent stories at Mount Hermon Baptist Church in New Orleans, Louisiana. God was a fierce force who fought with fire and water, and who had no match. God's son was matchless in a different way, a softer, kinder, gentler way. Together, greatness and great grace ruled and changed the world for the better. I think this is how I received it then. This is, in short, what I heard when I first heard the story. The story continued its sounding in me through Sunday school teachers like Kenneth Harrison, who taught the word, and choirs and soloists like Camille Harrison, who sang the word. I began reading biblical stories and books that focused on the story, like Fulton Sheen's *The Life of Christ*. I was caught up in preachers retelling the old biblical stories while adding newer stories that highlighted God's greatness and great grace in everyday life. Somehow I became convinced that I should and could join the band of storytellers, and I preached my first sermon a month shy of my becoming a teenager.

In the ensuing years, I developed a deepening relationship with the story. Along the way, at seminary, in church, and on the boulevards and side streets of life experience, I learned some sobering and sometimes uncomfortable truths: The story could be used in oppressive ways. The story has been and continues to be used to exclude the uninvited. Knowing the story and knowing God are two different matters. The story is open to interpretation and misinterpretation. No one can rightfully claim full and final comprehension of the story. Walter Rauschenbusch, the great Baptist social gospel preacher, once said that no church in any generation fully comprehends the saving work of God in Jesus Christ. The story is an ongoing, evolving narrative. My story, your story, our stories are vital parts of the continuing saga.

To preach the gospel is to take the baton of an old story and run with it for a while as it transforms and remakes itself in your hand and heart, even as you run with it. The story has life in it, and death. Indeed, the width and depth of its experience expanse is jazzlike. The gospel offers sufficient amounts of blues and swing, and a vast assortment of possibilities in between.

I love preaching, most of the time. I love the act of preaching, the physicality of it, the communal reality of it, the way I am completely absorbed in what I call the sweet spot of preaching, when all self-consciousness is gone, thinking seems effortless, and preacher and congregation are in sync in the same sacred moment. With all due respect to my affection for preaching, it is the story as opposed to the act of preaching that keeps me preaching. If I ever get over the story, I think I will stop preaching, maybe.

Personally speaking, mere preaching—the act of convincing oratory—may not be enough to keep me preaching. The story is what keeps me preaching: searching, saying, and singing. I think this is true in part due to my having pursued other outlets of creative expression, namely teaching and writing. The strengths of these communicative offerings are formidable, and rival those of preaching. Teaching offers an atmosphere of deliberate and sustained inquiry that preaching often does not match. Writing allows for more free play with new and sometimes threatening ideas, unlike preaching in which we often play and hear the same notes over and over again.

So in terms of method of communication, at this point in my life, preaching has serious competition. Moreover, after more than thirty years of preaching, I think I can live without preaching as a communicative discourse for a while simply because I have done so much of it. What I do not want to live without is preaching the gospel. The story urges me to stand and witness as though I am a preaching novice. The ever-expanding element of the gospel is what makes preaching so engaging. This is why preaching classes should allow sufficient time and inducement to taste and touch the story, to loiter about and within the story's inner and outer limits. Knowing the story is an unsung homiletical attribute. It is possible to unintentionally overfocus on preaching method and technique. Know the story and keep knowing it, and you'll find a way to tell it. Don't know the story, and the best techniques in the world will not keep you from coming up short as a gospel preacher.

I heard or read somewhere that prayer is not the reason for prayer, but that God is. Similarly, preaching is not the reason for preaching; God and gospel are the reasons for preaching. It is about telling the story and having the story tell us again and again, for the first time.

## Jazz and Preaching: Sweet Mysteries of Life

Jazz and preaching share the common ground of mystery. Both ultimately evade, to use poet David Whyte's phrase, "the cage of definition." People do conjure up acceptable working definitions of both. Definitions of jazz will usually include the words *African Americans* and *improvisation.* Preaching definitions tend to include *speech, persuasion,* and *gospel.* But the canons of definition for both realities witness to the element of the indescribable concerning both realities. There is a certain "beyond-ness" about the craft of which they speak. And one gets the impression that something of the critical essence of both jazz and preaching is in this incommunicable beyond-ness.

You hear it in Carrington's referring to jazz as a spirit that will not be bound by categories, and is always in pursuit, relentlessly progressing. Listen, and you can hear it when Billie Holiday says of her skill, "I don't think I'm singing. I feel like I am playing a horn."[14] I see it when I stare at one of my favorite jazz photographs.[15] Duke Ellington and Benny Goodman are sitting around a table in 1949, listening. Goodman is sitting back in his chair, content and mesmerized. Ellington's arms and hands are positioned like a church steeple beneath his chin. His face is that of a child's on Christmas morning. The woman singing is holding the mike close to her mouth. She is leaning into the song as the song leans into her. The lighting of the picture makes it appear that there is a star beneath her chin. Thanks to Herman Leonard, we have one of the most riveting pictures of Ella Fitzgerald, an extraordinary jazz spirit, that you will ever see. The picture captures not only the amazing person of the artist but also the arresting mystery of the artistry. The picture signals something of a cosmic nature about jazz.

I grew up feeling a certain cosmic, beyond-ness about preaching. Preachers hinted at it. Have you ever heard the expression "standin' in John's shoes"? While I was growing up, more often than not preachers prefaced their sermons with a reference to their standing in John's shoes. They were referring to the great river preacher of the Bible, John the Baptist. In this way, preachers were claiming their holy legacy, and the fact that what they were about to do was no mere casual conversation, but an event deeply rooted in time, the significance of which reached toward eternity. Sermon forewords usually included prayers that asked God to help preachers to do what they ultimately could not do alone. Preachers prayed that they would decrease so that God could increase. They prayed for God to "use them." They would pray for the Spirit "to come," "to stop by." When congregants joined the appeal and expectation, the result could be an extraordinary communal experience of enlightenment, inspiration, and healing.

The beyond-ness of preaching was evident in the preacher's public prayerful spirituality of preaching and in the articulated awareness that preaching was, ultimately, to borrow Reinhold Niebuhr's overused phrase, "an impossible possibility." There is the sense among some preachers that one is ever reaching, never fully and finally preaching. Who are we to think that we could ever hear God's word, let alone carry it to the ears of others? The weight of the presumption is overwhelming. Caesar Clark, a legend in black preaching circles, once said, "All of your life, preaching will tease you and taunt you. And when you come to the end, you will have to say that your preaching has been an embarrassed stammering."[16] Charles Booth, a premier revival preacher told me during an interview, "I feel like I have come up short. You know, it's very interesting. I have in my spirit preached on a level that I have never reached during the act of preaching." Similarly, Miles Davis spoke of hearing Dizzy Gillespie and Charlie Parker play together one night, and hearing something he had been trying to play ever since. Davis said, "I've gotten close, but not all the way there. I'm always looking for it, listening and feeling for it, though, trying to always feel it in and through the music I play every day."[17]

The mysterious common ground of jazz and preaching is this: one never ever *arrives*. Their wells are always deeper; there is always more. Where they are concerned, there is no period.

## Jazz and Preaching: Separations?

Are there places where jazz and preaching are more different than the same? I can think of a few possibilities. First, sometimes jazz musicians will play to themselves, to each other, or to the music. The audience appears ancillary. There is even a sense of acceptability and novelty about this. I remember hearing that Miles Davis sometimes played with his back facing the audience. This was more acceptable to some than to others. Many ardent jazz fans want their musicians to give undivided attention to the music. Such focus is where great music is found. For this kind of jazz fan the joy is in marveling at focused musicianship. Others believe that jazz lost its huge popularity when it lost its focus on the people, when it became less entertaining dance music and more artistic listening music. I attended a jazz concert recently, and it did appear as if the audience was remotely secondary to the accomplished trumpet player. His almost isolated endeavor had him making sounds with his horn that *he* wanted to hear. If the audience caught it, fine; if not, no harm done. There is in jazz a certain unqualified self-indulgence.

Gospel preaching can never be about word and the preacher only. Preaching is minimally a four-piece combo of God, message, messenger, and people. Each participant is an integral part of the preaching event. To disallow any one of these four definitive elements is to eliminate the preaching reality. The preacher does not have the option of preaching with his back toward the congregation, unless such posturing is part of an overall message intended to confront and communicate with the congregation.

Is there ever self-indulgence in preaching? Well, have you ever been so caught up in preaching that you were oblivious to the presence of anyone else, less out of disrespect and more from shear absorption? More than selfishness, I see this as being what writer Madeleine L'Engle refers to as "unself-consciousness":

> When we are *self*-conscious, we cannot be wholly aware; we must throw ourselves out first. This throwing ourselves away is the act of creativity. So, when we wholly concentrate, like a child in play, or an artist at work, then we share in the act of creating. We not only escape time, we also escape our self-conscious selves. . . . When we can play with the unself-conscious concentration of a child, this is: art: prayer: love.[18]

Maybe this is what the preachers I heard as a youth were seeking when they prayed before their sermons, "Lord, you increase while I decrease." They were praying to somehow lose themselves in the preaching moment. When this grace occurs, not a few congregants lose themselves as well, in the healing joy of the Lord. Individual surrender led to communal surrender.

A second seeming discontinuity between preaching and jazz may be in the area of understood ultimate objective. Would you say that the ultimate goal of gospel preaching is to persuade people to embrace God even as the gospel has embraced them in Christ Jesus? It is, is it not, to convince persons, in the words of Emilie Townes, that

we are not dipped
we are not sprinkled
we are not immersed
we are washed in the grace of God[19]

I doubt whether most jazz musicians would talk about the goal of jazz in this way. Based on my reading and conversations, jazz artists are more concerned with communicating as honestly as possible through their chosen creative expression what they hear. Often the word *freedom* is used to define the source, nature, and intention of the music. Such freedom is articulated in compelling and imaginative ways. Helio Orovio speaks of a drum sound that

vibrated between my hands, and
entered the center of the heart.[20]

While the self-understanding regarding the ultimate objectives of jazz and preaching may be different, there is a necessary convergence of their objectives. Divine love and freedom of expression share the same holy essence. Where there is no love, there can be no true freedom. Where there is no freedom, there can be no true love.

## Exercises and Resources

1. If you are a jazz fan, listen to two or three of your favorite CDs with the convergence of gospel preaching and jazz in mind. If you are new to jazz, purchase a jazz anthology CD like *Pure Jazz Encore!* (Verve, 2002). It features a variety of well-known jazz artists and selections. Some of the selections will appeal to you more than others. Listen with gospel preaching in mind. What do you hear?

2. Purchase and listen to Terri Lyne Carrington's *Jazz Is a Spirit*. Reflect on the connections and disconnections between jazz, gospel, preaching, and spirituality.

3. For a sound introduction to jazz, read part 1 of *Jazz 101* by John F. Szwed. *Jazz: A Crash Course*, by Simon Adams, is less comprehensive but offers sound general information in a portable and attractive format, and includes notable photographs and artwork.

4. For insight into the heart of jazz as an expression of African American pain, hope, and joy, read either or all of the following works: *Blues People*, by LeRoi Jones, *Living with Music*, by Ralph Ellison, and *The Spirituals and the Blues*, by James Cone.

5. Purchase or rent *Jazz*, a documentary film by Ken Burns. It will introduce you to the feelings and faces of jazz in ways that books simply cannot. The companion volume to this historic documentary is *Jazz: A History of America's Music*, by Geoffrey C. Ward and Ken Burns.

6. Listen to *Theology of the Blues* and *Jazz and Christianity* CDs, by Eugene L. Lowry. These are wonderful groundbreaking presentations on the shared history and experience of jazz and Christian faith.[21]

## Notes

1. Valerie Boyd, *Wrapped in Rainbows: The Life of Zora Neale Hurston* (New York: Scribner, 2003), 45.

2. Robert Jourdain, *Music, the Brain, and Ecstasy: How Music Captures Our Imagination* (New York: Avon Books, 1997), xii.

3. Carole Hand, *Jazz: A Journal with Paintings* (Rohnert, CA: Pomegranate Artbooks, 1993).

4. Kirk Byron Jones, *Rest in the Storm: Self-care Strategies for Clergy and Other Caregivers* (Valley Forge, PA: Judson Press, 2001), 73.

5. Gardner C. Taylor, "Eulogy to Sandy Ray," *The African American Pulpit* (Winter 2000–2001), 264.

6. Barbara Brown Taylor, *When God Is Silent* (Cambridge, MA: Cowley Publications, 1998), 74.

7. Abraham Joshua Heschel, *Moral Grandeur and Spiritual Audacity*, ed. Susannah Heschel (New York: The Noonday Press, 1996), 264.

8. Frederick Buechner, *Telling the Truth: The Gospel as Tragedy, Comedy, and Fairy Tale* (San Francisco: HarperSanFrancisco, 1977), 25.

9. Heschel, *Moral Grandeur and Spiritual Audacity*, 264.

10. James H. Cone, *The Spirituals and the Blues* (New York: The Seabury Press, 1972), 111.

11. Geoffrey C. Ward and Ken Burns, *Jazz: A History of America's Music* (New York: Alfred A. Knopf, 2000), 21.

12. Lara Pellegrinelli, "Singers, the SongBook, and Beyond," JVC Festival Program (2003), 22.

13. Geoffrey Himes, "Jazz Hymns, Catholic Tastes," *JazzTimes* (January–February 2002), 68-69.

14. Hand, *Jazz: A Journal with Paintings*.

15. Herman Leonard, "Duke Ellington and Benny Goodman Listen to Ella Fitzgerald," *Seeing Jazz: Artists and Writers on Jazz* (San Francisco: Chronicle Books, 1997), 93.

16. Bruce Nolan, "Master of Oratory Fills Pews at Revival," *The Times Picayune* (June 9, 1995), B-2.

17. Jon Michael Spencer, "Miles Davis' Kind of Blue," *Theology Today* (January 1996), 508.

18. Madeleine L'Engle, *Glimpses of Grace* (San Francisco: HarperSanFrancisco, 1996), 162-63.

19. Emilie M. Townes, *In a Blaze of Glory* (Nashville: Abingdon Press, 1995), 47.

20. Helio Orovio, "The Cord Between the Fingers," *Seeing Jazz*, 18.

21. To purchase CDs you may call 816-333-4506, or e-mail elowry7000@aol.com.

CHAPTER THREE

# Dreaming a Song, Hearing a Sermon

*It is not the ear that hears, it is not the physical organ that performs that act of inner receptivity. It is the total person who hears.*

—M. C. Richards, *Centering: In Pottery, Poetry, and the Person*

*I don't write out of what I know; I write out of what I wonder.*

—Lucille Clifton

## Dreaming, Listening, and Squinting

Even if you do not choose to rent or purchase Burns's documentary on jazz, there is a clip that you absolutely must see. It is a brief segment called "Dreaming" on episode 5: "Swing: Pure Pleasure." As the segment commences you hear mellow piano playing in the background. Then, Edward Kennedy "Duke" Ellington appears seated at a piano. Composer of over three thousand songs, pianist and bandleader Ellington is widely regarded as one of the two or three most influential figures in the history of jazz. Gifted with heaping portions of confidence and poise, Ellington's personality complemented his musical genius. Here is a transcript of "Dreaming":

> *[There is piano playing in the background and then silence.]*
>
> UNIDENTIFIED INTERVIEWER: Where did you get your ideas from?
>
> ELLINGTON: *[Ellington has his left hand on his left ear, in a relaxed, reflective posture.]* Ideas? Oh, man, I got a million dreams. That's all I do is dream. All the time.
>
> INTERVIEWER: I thought you played piano.
>
> ELLINGTON: Nooo! This is not piano; this is dreaming.
>
> *[Ellington begins playing slowly. He looks off camera and suddenly the sound of soft playing on a cymbal is heard under Ellington's notes. A bass player on camera opts to sit still and observe Ellington's extemporaneous playing. At one point, Ellington squints his eyes and leans toward the piano in search of an elusive chord he ultimately locates. He pauses for a moment.]*
>
> ELLINGTON: That's dreaming.
>
> *[Ellington continues to play.]*

This clip is striking to me for several reasons. First, I am taken with Ellington's denial: he does not play the piano; he dreams. What an astounding self-understanding that comes off as being thoroughly genuine. It is not as much about the piano as it is about the dream that the piano sounds, interprets, and articulates. The piano and the pianist for that matter are conduits, servants to an unseen, intangible influence that Ellington is comfortable referring to as a dream.

Ellington's confession brings to mind an experience shared by the writer Annie Dillard. It, coincidentally, involves a dream. In *The Writing Life*, Dillard recalls a dream she had when she was learning, with limited success, how to split wood:

> I had a dream in which I was given to understand, by the powers that be, how to split wood. You aim, said the dream—of course!—at the chopping block. It is true. You aim at the chopping block, not at the wood; then you split the wood, instead of chipping it. You cannot do the job cleanly unless you treat the wood as the transparent means to an end, by aiming past it.[1]

Ellington's dreaming is a way of aiming past the piano. What he is after or what is after him is (with all due respect to Steinway) something that ultimately transcends the piano. The end result, however, is piano playing of the highest order.

I wonder when Ellington began to feel that playing the piano was something deeper than playing the piano. I want to ask him if he felt this way every time he played. I want to ask him about his perception of the difference between "dreaming piano playing" and "nondreaming piano playing."

The second striking element about this film clip is that listening appears to be at the center of Ellington's dreaming. It is noteworthy that the segment begins with Ellington covering one of his ears. When he plays, dreams, the left hand comes down and he is all ears. His listening is visible, purposeful, and intense. As you observe him in the film, you can almost hear him listening. Ellington's listening is accented by the sparseness of musical notes. In his impromptu performance, there is just as much silence as there is sound. Although the silences are rests in musical terms, in reality Ellington is not resting in such spaces. He is hard at work listening, at one point successfully searching for a hidden but heard sound.

Ellington speaks of having a million dreams. I may not have a million questions about his listening, but I have more than a few, including:

- What is listening?
- How do you listen?
- What helps you listen?
- What gets in the way of your listening?
- How do you know when you've heard the right sound?
- To what extent do you hear a sound already made/formed?
- To what extent do you help make the sound that you hear?
- What is it to hear a wrong note?
- What is the source of what you hear?
- Are there times when you can't listen?
- How much is listening influenced by internal realties such as mood, and external factors such as setting?
- Do you always play what you hear?

- How does it feel to play before or without listening?
- Are there different levels of listening?
- Is listening a gift or a skill that can be nurtured and cultivated?

There is Ellington's dreaming, listening, and squinting. Ellington listens and feels what he hears. He is feeling to hear, and hearing to feel. As profound as his dreaming and listening are, the most enticing moment of the film clip is Ellington's squinting to hear and play a chord. When I see him squinting, I see the following, in no particular order: reaching, longing, choosing, losing, pursuing, deciding, and perhaps hurting. Some notes are harder to hear; some notes require that we give up something of ourselves that they might become "heard-able."

Up to the point of squinting, Ellington's playing is flowing and unhindered. When he squints, for the first time discord becomes a real possibility. He can hear and he can *not* hear and barely hear and "mis-hear." Listening is not always effortless and easy. Hearing is harder at some times than it is at other times, and sometimes listening involves ordeal, strain, and pathos.

Ellington's squinting tells me that he is not a mere eavesdropper in the music-making process. Perhaps the squinting hints at the mystery of creativity, the calling not to just play the sound that you hear, but to help make the sound itself. To be coparticipant in the construction of a sound never heard before, a brand new sound. Could it be that when Ellington squints, we are seeing the visible manifestation of his not only hearing the music but also his helping to create music?

## Hearing the Call

When and where I grew up in New Orleans, Louisiana, church people talked about a person needing to be "called to preach." One didn't just start preaching (although many were accused of doing just that), but in the tradition of Moses, Mary, and Saul, you had to have an experience of God asking you or calling you forth to bear the word. As I look back on it, my experience was more of a succession of experiences than a singular memorable event. I can remember sitting under a tree in our backyard for hours looking up at the sky and sensing connection with it and beyond. I would look, feel, and listen. And then there were the nights. Many evenings, as a boy, I lay in my bed unable to start sleep or go back to sleep. I wondered about things and felt a presence that compelled me toward religious reality. Sometimes this frightened me; it never stopped drawing me. Such experiences led me to my parents and then to my pastor and church, professing a call to preach. I preached my first sermon a month shy of my thirteenth birthday.

Subsequently, I have learned that preaching does not have a monopoly on sacred calling. Gregg Levoy writes in what may be the best book ever written on the subject, *Callings: Finding and Following an Authentic Life*:

> Few people actually receive big calls, in visions of flaming chariots and burning bushes. Most of the calls we receive and ignore are the proverbial still, small voices that the biblical prophets heard, the daily calls to pay attention to our intuitions, to be authentic, to live by our own codes of honor.[2]

We are all mysteriously compelled to vocational expressions of some sort. We feel and hear our callings in different ways, but we are all called continuously.

The formation of the preacher of the gospel begins with the act of listening to the call to preach. The central undoing of preaching is that we do not carry over this fundamental action of listening into our ministries. When listening is lost, we become fixated on the saying element of preaching. Preaching becomes first and last persuasive speech making. I object. Preaching is not *saying* first. Preaching is, as it is for jazz, a matter of *listening* first. The preaching life, as is the poet's life, is a life of listening. Listening is the supreme action, listening with mind and soul.

The call is but the first of several hearings that the preacher must attend to before she or he reaches hearing the sermon. There are other antecedent, ongoing hearings that provide the resonance for preaching, the tonal quality of spiritual integrity. Before and as the preacher hears sermon, she or he must hear Spirit, life, and gospel. Along with calling, hearing Spirit, life, and gospel are the necessary preliminary and ongoing processional hearings of preaching. The ability to hear is a gift. Wanting to hear, which I am using synonymously for listening in this instance, and actually hearing are choices.

Listening, not saying, is the vital nerve of preaching. If you can't hear it, you can't say it.

## Hearing Spirit

> Every time I hear the Spirit moving in my heart, I will pray.

> Every time I hear the Spirit moving in my heart, I will pray.

So sings the chorus of a Negro spiritual. To hear the Spirit is to risk intimacy with God. We are talking about an ineffable reality, so we must admit and remember that all discussion falls short in every way. But our inability to finely comprehend and articulate spiritual intimacy does not negate its reality. Complicated and dangerous as it is, accepting the reality of spiritual intimacy, hearing and knowing God, is crucial for the gospel preacher.

If Madeleine L'Engle and James Washington are right, encountering God is a crucial and scary prospect for most of us, even the churchiest among us. In *A Scholar's Benediction*, Washington prays on our behalf, "[God] we are afraid of you."[3] In *Glimpses of Grace*, L'Engle offers, "We build churches which are the safest possible places in which to escape God."[4] When I mistakenly type s-c-a-r-e-d for s-a-c-r-e-d, is it simply because the words are formed with the same six letters, or is something else at work?

What is it to hear God? No one can say conclusively on this side of Jordan. In the now of life, I know that hearing God has something to do with silence. Not that silence has a monopoly on God. I hear God in the joyous celebration of children romping in a park. But silence is a mysterious gate to dimensions of God we may not be able to access otherwise. The bareness of silence demands that I loosen and lose the garments of presumptions and assumptions about God. In silence I am more likely to experience God on God's terms and not my own. In silence I am less likely to sidestep mystery.

To hear God is to gain a tolerance for my own acceptance, to accept that I am accepted. It is not uncommon for African American church organizations to offer monetary gifts to guest worship leaders at special services held to celebrate the group's founding. The offerings are usually modest, covering travel expenses and a little more. The amount is larger for the guest speaker. I remember preaching at such a service. Toward the end of worship, gifts were handed out. To my alarm, an uncomfortable pattern emerged. One after another, guest participants said in essence "Thanks, but no thanks," and "honorably" handed the offering back to the person making the presentation. This was truly uncomfortable for me because our second child had just been born, I was in school, and we needed the money. *What should I do?* When the moment of truth came, what I did was tell the truth: "With all due respect to the kind gestures of the recipients who have gone before me, I cannot follow in their footsteps. We have just had a child, and I am in a doctoral program. Your kind generosity is accepted in the spirit in which it is given." The laughter was loud and loving.

Accepting God's unconditional love may be the hardest acceptance of all, and the most important. Hearing God is accepting the sacred proposal of unearned and unending blazing affection. It is to not only become aware of God's love afresh, but to receive and even revel in this mighty love.

To hear God is to practice tenacious openness. It is to travel in a land beyond our hearing. In a way, hearing God requires a necessary deftness, an empty openness to a reality that, on the one hand, human ears cannot begin to comprehend, and, on the other hand, human essence has been granted wondrous access. Hearing God is *knowing* and *not knowing* at the same time; it is clarity shrouded in mystery.

I suspect we give the foregoing little attention in most preaching classes. Yet the essential touchstone of gospel preaching is daring to hear, individually and collectively, the mystery from which the gospel emerges. To this end, perhaps all preaching classes should begin and end with extended moments of personal and communal silence. The mysterious compelling power of preaching is abiding in the Abiding Spiritual Presence. In his book *Preaching with Freshness*, Bruce Mawhinney refers to this as the "reservoir power" of preaching:

> "Preachers ought to be more like great reservoirs than mere water pipes. They should operate out of the fullness of God's presence in their lives rather than operating on the margin."[5]

## Hearing Life

The disciples are ready. They have sat with the stranger-turned-teacher for weeks. He has inspired them with his story style of instruction and his stirring vision for a new community. Moreover, they are becoming increasingly convinced that he has the strength of will to pull it off, to make of their old world a new world. One by one, they commit to joining his movement, or at least to start out with him. The day arrives for their first ministry initiative. They sit mobilized; the hours pass and they go nowhere. Finally, Jesus says. "Okay, we are ready to move out. First stop, a wedding feast." Thus, the world's greatest mission initiative begins with ordinary people in the celebrative atmosphere of everyday life.

The ministry of Jesus is organic, intrinsically connected to mustard seed, lamp stands, bushel baskets, children on laps, women at wells, and men in trees. He does not run by life on the way to his mission. His mission *is* life—ordinary life, drinking water; and extraordinary life, walking on water. The stuff and style of his sermonizing comes from the soil of living. He knows that God's noticing and our noticing the color purple in a field (with gratitude to Alice Walker) are comparable notes in the same sacred song.

To run by life is to run by gospel preaching: speaking Reality to reality. To not hear, touch, smell, savor, and at times even curse life is to not preach, in the words of contemporary jazz artist Lizz Wright, with "the salt in the stew." In its bitterness and sweetness, life is the salt, sugar, and all the spices in between of preaching. Life, not abstraction or illusion, is where Jesus started, ended, and started up again.

*What have you to do with life, preacher? Preacher, what has life to do with you?*

Listening to life involves listening to one's own life. The essential prerequisite action is having a life to listen to. Alas, many well-meaning preachers have lost their lives to their professional roles. They have allowed themselves to become revered dead people walking. Like the pseudoclergyperson in Alice Walker's *By the Light of My Father's Smile*, their lives have been "sucked into the black cloth."

In order to listen to our lives we must give ourselves permission to have lives apart from ecclesiastical existence and ministerial functioning. Lively, real preaching has a better chance of coming forth from lively persons who dare to be real within and without their clergy clothes. To push this further: many ministers have unconsciously maimed their preaching by making idols of their roles and ministries. Their ministry, not God, has become the ultimate object of their attention and energy, to the detriment of deepening spirituality, family relationships, and personal wellness. This truth must stand face-to-face with another: God never wills that we live for idols, let alone die for them. Besides, persons make far better preachers than statues.

## Hearing Gospel

I am making a case for preliminary, ongoing hearings prior to listening in for the sermon. Another first lingering listening is listening to the gospel. What is the gospel to you? Please answer in simple, direct language initially. It need not be a wordy answer. M. C. Richards once wrote a poem consisting of just two words.[6]

When I speak of hearing the gospel, I mean somehow being in touch with the Spirit, the journey, and destination of the gospel, the beating heart of the Word. Without the gospel sound, we run the risk of telling disjointed hit-and-miss stories on Sunday morning. To hear the heartbeat of the gospel is to feel a sense of sacred continuity and purpose about it all.

What is the central theme of the gospel? Preaching titan Gardner Taylor says it is God trying to get back what is God's.[7] Sometimes I come across a poet's or novelist's phrase that sounds close to what I hear to be near the heart of the gospel:

> But there it was again, percolating up through the layers of years, bubbling out at Martha's feet like a perverse spring. This sly and relentless force that moved through the world, this patient and brutal something that people called hope.[8]

In her poem "My Friend Yeshi," Alice Walker speaks of "the true wine of astonishment": our not being over even when things are at their worst.[9]

Amos, Mary, and Jesus are more direct about the purpose of *Insistent Love*:

> Let justice roll down like water, and righteousness like a mighty stream.
>
> —Amos 5:24 (NKJV)

> "He has brought down the powerful from their thrones."
>
> —Luke 1:52

> "He has sent me to proclaim release to the captives."
>
> —Luke 4:18

All of the foregoing singers and dreamers join in cosmic imagining. Such imaginings are the verbal and nonverbal responses to, in the words of preaching professor Thomas Troeger, the gospel touching the preacher's own life.[10] Listen long enough, and somewhere in the hearing we become cocreators, players, with the Creative Source who ignites and invites our imagining. It is not just a matter of listening to the music; when it comes to gospel preaching, we are invited to help actively construct the gospel telling. This compels from us a choice to listen, to imagine, and to create.

I write by candlelight; the flame inspires me. As I finished a writing session one morning, I made a startling discovery—a broken unstruck match lying near my left hand. I noticed as well that the candle was not burning. That morning I had not lit the candle; I had not used the match. To preach the gospel without listening to calling, Spirit, life, and gospel is to preach without the flame, to preach with an unstruck match.

## Exercises and Resources

1. Begin journaling, freely expressing your deepest and wildest ponderings on life.

2. Buy a box of crayons and medium- or large-sized drawing paper. Begin your sermon preparation by drawing pictures of your ideas. Give yourself permission to image your sermon, especially at the outset, without limits and in living color. Use crayons or colored pencils to create pictures of important meanings of the gospel for you. The crayons and colored pencils will help lift you out of an overly cognitive apprehension of the gospel and into a childlike, more holistic engagement. How does the gospel feel in your heart, on your hands, and between your toes?

3. Read poetry paying attention to the visions set off inside you. Notice the power of speech to open you up, and to widen the terrain of existence.

4. Read children's books. Become reacquainted with your innate imagination and dream consciousness. Nicholas Allan's *Jesus' Day Off* will prove beneficial to you beyond preaching.

5. Pay attention to your indirect sermon preparation, the way preaching material comes to you during your leisure, when the sermon is the last thing on your mind. (The worst thing you can do with a sermon is think about it too much.)

6. Observe more silence. In silence, alternative forms of knowing other than hard cognition are operative. Silence is a way of making yourself receptive and supple for soft knowing, for spiritual insight, for mystery.

NOTES

1. Annie Dillard, *The Writing Life* (New York: Harper & Row, 1989), 43.

2. Gregg Levoy, *Callings: Finding and Following an Authentic Life* (New York: Three Rivers Press, 1998), 5.

3. James Melvin Washington, *Conversations with God: Two Centuries of Prayers by African Americans* (New York: HarperCollins, 1994), 285.

4. L'Engle, *Glimpses of Grace*, 247.

5. Bruce Mawhinney, *Preaching with Freshness* (Eugene, OR: Harvest House, 1991), 133.

6. M. C. Richards, *Centering: In Pottery, Poetry, and the Person* (Hanover, NH: Wesleyan University Press, 1962), 69.

7. "The Sweet Torture of Sunday Morning," Interview with Gardner C. Taylor, *Leadership* (Summer Quarter 1981), 20.

8. Pam Durban, "Soon," in *The Best American Short Stories, 1997*, ed. E. Annie Proulx (Boston: Houghton Mifflin, 1997), 263.

9. Alice Walker, *Absolute Trust in the Goodness of the Earth* (New York: Random House, 2003), 145.

10. Thomas H. Troeger, *Imagining a Sermon* (Nashville: Abingdon Press, 1990), 75.

CHAPTER FOUR

# A Call to Create

*Creative courage . . . is the discovering of new forms, new symbols, new patterns on which new society can be built. Every profession can and does require some creative courage.*

—Rollo May, *The Courage to Create*

*What we have to express is already with us,* is *us, so the work of creativity is not a matter of making the material come, but of unblocking the obstacles to its natural flow.*

—Stephen Nachmanovitch

My Saturday evening experience with Ella Fitzgerald's singing introduced me to the emotive power of jazz. Looking back, this was a rediscovery of sorts. When I was a child, I began doing an impersonation of a famous person whose voice was unlike anyone else's I had ever heard. I would drop my voice as low as I could get it, put some gruff into it and then say-sing "Hello, dolly; it's so nice to have you back where you belong." Most of you know I was doing an impression of jazz forefather Louis Armstrong. Jazz was with me from the beginning; I just didn't realize it.

Along with the emotional power and shear compelling attraction of the music, a third attribute of jazz, quite honestly, makes me somewhat jealous of jazz artists. Scratch the *somewhat.* I am at times insanely jealous of jazz musicians when it comes to their radical acceptance of creativity.

On the heels of my Saturday evening deliverance, I began purchasing jazz recordings. I was amazed at what I heard. I was enamored with hearing so many different sounds from a vast assortment of instruments and voices, including instruments that sounded like voices, and voices that sounded like instruments. They were sounds I had never heard before. I was amazed that they could be connected and disconnected in so many different ways.

I began noticing and naming what was appealing to me: precise sound, tone, and nuance; diversity of rhythm and beat. The blending of carefulness and playfulness displayed by the musicians grabbed me and would not let me go. I learned the names of the acknowledged masters of several instruments, and the identities of some of the great vocalists on leave from heaven.

Listening to a new CD by one of these extraordinary artists became an event for me. Sometimes I would play a selection over and over again to hear the song or to hear a particular section in a song, a stunning sound combination. As I began to collect more and more music, I began noticing how a singular song could be interpreted and presented so differently by artists. Sounds, patterns of sounds, nuances, tones, shades of tones, songs, song derivations, musical gifts, skills, and charms! It was as if I had suddenly landed on a new planet. I soon discovered that the planet was dependent on a regulating vitalizing energy—*creativity*.

## The Creative Rights of Jazz

Listen to several jazz artists talk about their impressions of jazz-making:

> When I play, I search around inside until I hear something that feels right. [My] aesthetic involves making every note count and striving to play notes that I have not played before.[1]
>
> —Marc Copland, pianist

> I try to hear it through the guitar first, fine-tuning and experimenting, and then just build a house—a musical house for a song to live in. It's a matter of experimenting with the melody, creating a harmony, creating a mood and creating a tempo. In a sense you're building a home, or a vessel, for that emotion, lyrical phrase or story.[2]
>
> —Cassandra Wilson, vocalist

> At one time I could hear a musician playing and could hear the note he was going to make next.... It was just that fast, just like telling someone's fortune; it may have something to do with the fastness of the mind and hearing.... I think it's useful in your music. You can't control it. You see these things when you're not even expecting them.[3]
>
> —Mary Lou Williams, pianist

> When you're workin' the spirit understands that you are serious and that you are preparing yourself to receive that information. Stay in the state of preparedness. Coltrane said that. You got to stay in the state of preparedness all the time.[4]
>
> —Wynton Marsalis, trumpeter

preach about Jesus who was, in biblical parlance, "the same yesterday, today, and tomorrow." Unfortunately, the same description could be applied to some of their preaching. Inadvertently, the same old story led to the same old telling.

Even if one grants a sense of sameness and even finality to God's redemptive work in Christ Jesus, it is always possible to widen our vision of God's labor of grace. We can regularly preach new dimensions of the "unchanged" faith experience, and preach it in novel ways. Even if you must believe that the word has not changed, you must grant that our apprehension of the word is constantly changing, and the Word behind the word has never been fully comprehended. What if after two thousand years of preaching we have yet to scratch the surface in terms of comprehending and construing ways of telling the story? What if God is waiting with tiptoe-expectancy for us to creatively see and seize these new ways?

## Unleashing the Creative Impulse

Creativity in preaching begins with lavish portions of personhood and permission.

Human beings are an extraordinarily creative species. The trouble is that most of us never approach the vast expanse of our creative capacities. Scientists tell us that we use only 10 percent of our mental capacity. Most of us sleep with our creative limitation. We are discouraged daily by crushing societal reminders of what we cannot do. The first step in becoming a more creative preacher is embracing your status as a creative individual. The proof of your creative genius is not in your ability to paint stunning pictures or write stirring musical compositions, but in your ability to imagine and playfully construct. To the extent that all of us can imagine and make, we all are creative—most of us to a measure beyond our wildest dreams.

Creativity flourishes when we dare to be, freely and fully, our genuinely creative selves. Creative preaching, free and insightful sermonizing, comes more easily and regularly from free people. Free people are those who have accepted their acceptance from God and life. Having received this fundamental acceptance, they are free to route their energies into creative expression as opposed to constructing personal and interpersonal defenses and denials: the fatiguing work we do when we are not at home with who we are.

Owning your capacity to create must be followed by granting yourself permission to do so. Here is where the jazz musician is such a wonderful model for the preacher. Who authorized Louis Armstrong to play with such passion, precision, and power? And who gave him the permission to put gravel in his voice and sing in a way that no one had sung before? What gave Sarah Vaughan the right to assume that her voice was no less an instrument than Armstrong's trumpet? How dare she have the audacity to think that she could master control over her voice in the same way that a musician honorably tames and rides her instrument? Where did such creative authorization derive? The authority came from Within and Without, the former being no less sacred than the latter. Receiving permission for creative preaching means believing that the Spirit is delighted with our daring to hear and tell the gospel in fresh new ways, in ways that cause God to smile.

Once, as I was observing morning devotion, I began stretching my arm forward to get some of the waking-up kinks out. I did this several times. The last time I stretched forth my arm I realized that I was moving it toward the place where a small candle sat burning. When it comes to creativity, the great challenge is to reach for the flame, to embrace the fire.

## Four Essential Attributes for Cultivating Creativity

### *Curiosity*

Curiosity is one of the unsung gifts of the Spirit. If there is an instant when creativity is buried inside of us it is the moment we ask the question "Why?" for the last time. Do not set out to become a more curious preacher. Become a more curious person in your work and leisure and all the living places in between, and simply allow this inquiring attitude free passage into your preaching preparation and performance. You will know you are offering sufficient access to curiosity when, among a million and one other proofs, you are as concerned about what a text does not say as what it says; when the white fire (the empty spaces) of the Bible and your notes or manuscript matter as much to you as the print; when you interpret textual challenges as adventures more than problems; and when you are as interested in what people may hear as you are in what you will say.

Curiosity is not a path for those addicted to comfort. Difference is often initially experienced as intrusion. I appreciate Peter Berger's descriptive phrase for assaults on our familiarities: creative cognitive dissonance. Though curiosity may leave you without rest, it will never leave you without growth. Gregg Levoy offers:

> One of the shining qualities that heroes possess is the willingness to be educated by all things. They learn from the most impressive variety of people and experiences:

> the wise and the foolish; the obvious and the inconceivable; the living and the dead; the things they love and the things they hate; children and animals and the voluble energetics of nature; all the thumpings and all the bounties they earn from the world. "*Everything* nourished him," Henry Miller once said of Goethe.[5]

## *Openness*

A jazz pianist once spoke of being so open in his practicing that he at points deliberately made ugly sounds so that he would be open to everything.

Creativity needs open space to skip and jump, and prance and dance. Most of us are not use to living with mental, emotional, and spiritual spaciousness. Our inner lives are crammed and cramped with presumptions and preferences. In order to have more space we will have to loosen our grasp on entrenched understandings that make us feel powerful and in control. This is the tender place of one of our greatest fears, what Anthony DeMello refers to as the fear of the loss of the known. Yet authentic openness demands that we feel the fear and venture out into the deep waters of new beliefs anyway. This is a choice to be vulnerable: valiantly open to new experiences and insights. The dearth of such things is due less to their reality and more to our closeted, closed minds.

Openness speaks to the importance of "never arriving" as a preacher. Jon Pearles recalls this quality in the person of the late great jazz vocalist Joe Williams:

> His vocal style was changing. When he began singing, he often performed without amplification, belting above the band. But during his years with the [Count] Basie band, he listened to tape recordings of his nightly performances, and he honed his style, paring away nonessentials, improving his intonation and adding new subtleties. His

> role with the Basie band was as a blues singer, but he was increasingly drawn to ballads.[6]

Williams never "arrived"; he was constantly evolving. He remained open.

## *Risks*

Preaching is playing with fire. It is no wonder that the first biblical call to someone to speak forth on behalf of God involves a bush that burns and burns and burns. Preaching is a fiery reality—apart from emotional oratorical styling. Preaching like we are fighting a swarm of bees has nothing to do with the fire that I am talking about. I am referring to an innate fire. A fire that has less to do with *who* the preacher is and *how* he or she preaches, and more to do with *that* he or she preaches in the first place.

What is the innate fire of preaching? Preaching's impulse is set right smack in the middle of the mystery of God. We preach, first, not because we have something to say, but because God has something to say. There is fire there: God, Loving Spirit, has something to say. Annie Dillard retells this splendid story in *The Writing Life*:

> "Rebbe Shmelke of Nickolsberg, it was told, never really heard his teacher, the Maggid of Mezritch, finish a thought because as soon as the latter would say 'and the Lord spoke,' Shmelke would begin shouting in wonderment, 'The Lord spoke, the Lord spoke,' and continue shouting until he had to be carried from the room."[7]

Wow!

There is fire in the sacred initiative, and there is fire in the essential divine declaration:

YOU ARE LOVED

YOU ARE BLESSED

YOU ARE ACCEPTED

There is yet another element to the flame: the saying and hearing of words, something we tend to take for granted because of the frequency with which we speak and the prevalence of manipulative communication. Still, saying and hearing are wondrous realties. To say is to send forth breath. Right now, place one of your hands a few inches from your mouth and say something, anything. Feel the air, the breath? Biblical wisdom has traditionally taught that our breath and our spirits are intertwined. We can never send out anything verbally without sending something from our spirit. Every time you speak, no matter what you say, your spirit goes forth. Thus the admonition "Be careful what you say" takes on greater meaning.

Hearing is no less amazing. Hearing is letting the spirits in, and subjecting ourselves to the possibilities of alteration and transformation. That's risky, fiery stuff. Have you ever heard the warning "You can't listen to everything"? This is why when a capable speaker engages an open audience, sparks fly. Just a few weeks ago I sat in an orientation program for high school students and parents. Twelve or more school representatives briefed us on what to expect during the new academic year. Most of the speakers were very good. One speaker, the athletic director, was exceptional. He spoke clearly, confidently, and with noticeable passion. He concluded by saying, sending, "We ARE the MUSTANGS, and we ARE going to have a GREAT year!" The energy level in the room shot up dramatically.

Communication is about sending and receiving who we are and who we are becoming. It is about pouring out our essence and our emergence. Communication is a deeply spiritual undertaking, no matter what we say.

How serendipitous! My marvelous, merrymaking wife, Bunnie, walked into the room and asked if she could interrupt for a moment. She usually doesn't bother me when I am writing, graciously offering me the gift of space. I turned to listen, knowing it must be important. Smiling, she began describing a dream she had the night before in which I was climbing a tall pole. In her dream she grew concerned that I was nearing some wires. She became afraid that I would touch the wires and be electrocuted. She called out to me, but I kept climbing. Suddenly, I grabbed the wires and began to swing on them without bringing harm to myself.

Preaching is a daring enterprise involving mystery, monumental message, and the amazing reality of communication. In preaching, we risk embarrassment and failure; but to preach is to take such risks in sacrifice and delight.

How dare you?

I dare you!

## *Grace*

Nothing stunts freedom of imagination and expression more in preaching, or any other pursuit for that matter, than the fear of messing up, of blowing it, of embarrassing ourselves. In fact, the fear of public speaking is the greatest fear among adults, even greater than the fear of death. Fear keeps us from taking creative risks. Fear sucks life and creative expression out of us, leaving us dry and dull. Fearful preaching, if it preaches at all, is boring, fixated, predictable sermonizing, at best. The answer to the fear of new creative pursuits is grace. Grace says to fear, "You know what, you've got a point. This new thing I am attempting may leave me flat on my face. But that's all right. Chances are my malady will not be a sickness unto death, and I'll live to learn from it, and maybe, wonder of wonders, even laugh about it." Do you want to be more creative in your preaching life and life in general? Advance yourself large portions of God's amazing grace. Maybe the most amazing thing of all about grace is that we don't take as much of it as we can and should.

## Exercises and Resources

Create your creativity! I mean this very literally. Although we have discussed some basic rules of creativity, in a very real sense, when it comes to individual human expression there are no rules. Nachmanovitch's words are true: "The creative processes of one are not the same as those of another. . . . Each of us must find his or her own way into and through these essential mysteries."[8]

That having been said, for sure the creative preacher is ever widening her or his knowledge of sermonic options. The creative preacher is less and less afraid of having an experimental disposition. Imagine new preaching vistas and prospects for yourself and then create your creativity, beginning with the way you prepare to preach. Use the following exercises to get you started.

### *Presermon Creativity (Endless List #1)*

1. Work together with several colleagues on a common text.

2. Purchase and begin studying new biblical commentaries. Have a dialogue with the writers. Ask questions. Argue.

3. Read a short story each week related or unrelated to your message. This is a good way to develop a deepening appreciation for communicative precision, pacing, and climax.

4. Read and speak poetry. There is no better and more fulfilling way to develop a deepening appreciation for words and spaces.

5. Read anything and everything. Reading fills your well. It may also create an ease with the process of communication.

6. Observe standup comics. This is a fun way to appreciate the homiletically unheralded importance of timing as it relates to speech effectiveness. You may want to learn and practice the fine art of telling a joke.

7. Speaking of films, go to the theater or watch movies at home. Good film directors are master storytellers. Films also tread in the waters of the impulses, drives, desires, pains, and joys of what it means to be alive.

8. Be alert to life. Chart how much of your sermon comes from purposeful planning and how much comes from paying more attention to life.

9. Keep a notebook or index cards at the ready.

10. Purchase a portable tape recorder and travel with it.

11. Collage your sermon. As part of your preparation, cut and paste pictures of images that you think are important to your message.

12. Watch cartoons. Creators of cartoons are some of the most creative people on earth.

13. Initiate a conversation about a sermon point with a complete stranger. Strangers may offer a slant on something you have not considered.

14. Think of three ways you can be more experimental (do something different) in the following prepreaching areas:

(a) selecting subjects/themes/titles
(b) choosing objectives
(c) selecting words, phrases, sentences
(d) conceptualizing beginnings, developments, conclusions

### *Sermon Creativity (Endless List #2)*

1. Try preaching in the first person, and other ways of living in the text.

2. Alternate between preaching with and without notes/manuscript.

3. Be open to last-minute and on-the-spot additions and deletions. A sermon is never finally and fully constructed in the study. We continue to make the sermon as we preach it and in ruminating conversations thereafter.

4. Be more open to what the preaching moment offers your preaching by way of setting, sounds, moods, faces, and surprises.

5. Vary your sermon lengths. Great sermons come in all sorts of time lengths. It's not how long it is. (I once heard a story concerning the lauded jazz pianist Count Basie. On one occasion, another stellar pianist Oscar Peterson was playing before him and inadvertently began playing Count Basie's theme song. When he realized what he'd done, Peterson was deeply embarrassed. As soon as he exited the stage he began apologizing to the elder keyboard virtuoso. Basie simply nodded and walked over to the piano for his set. Peterson said Basie slowly and gently played two notes, and, with those minute meticulous nuanced musical sounds, washed away any memory of Peterson's performance. Two notes!)

6. Purchase anything at all by pianist Cyrus Chestnut. (His 2003 CD *You Are My Sunshine* will do just fine.) Listen. Listen. Listen. Seek to emulate in your preaching, in your unique way, his communicative touch, dexterity, honesty, and joy.

7. Think of three ways you can be more experimental (do something different) in the following preaching areas:

(a) saying words, phrases, sentences
(b) using and varying volume, tones, and rhythms
(c) exercising pacing and pausing
(d) telling stories

## *Creativity Reading Suggestions*

Brenda Ueland, *If You Want to Write: A Book About Art, Independence, and Spirit* (Saint Paul, MN: Graywolf Press, 1997).

Rollo May, *The Courage to Create* (New York: W. W. Norton & Company, 1994).

Robert Wuthnow, *Creative Spirituality: The Way of the Artist* (Berkeley: University of California Press, 2003).

Matthew Fox, *Creativity: Where the Divine and the Human Meet* (New York: J. P. Tarcher, 2002).

Linda Schierse Leonard, *The Call to Create: Celebrating Acts of Imagination* (New York: Harmony Books, 2000).

Twyla Tharp, *The Creative Habit: Learn It and Use It for Life* (New York: Simon & Schuster, 2003).

## NOTES

1. Bill Milkowski, "Hearsay," *JazzTimes* (October 2002), 22.
2. John Berlau, "All That Jazz, and Then Some," *USA Weekend* (June 21-23, 2002), 16.
3. Linda Dahl, *Morning Glory: A Biography of Mary Lou Williams* (New York: Pantheon Books, 1999), 9.
4. Touré, "Wynton Marsalis," *Icon Thoughtstyle Magazine*.
5. Gregg Levoy, *Callings*, 99.
6. Jon Pearles, Joe Williams obituary, *The New York Times* (March 31, 1999).
7. Dillard, *The Writing Life*, 35.
8. Stephen Nachmanovitch, *Free Play: Improvisation in Life and Art* (New York: Tarcher/Putnam, 1990), 10.

CHAPTER FIVE

# The Freedom of Improvisation

*If you are playing jazz, you have to play what comes out at any given moment.*

—John Coltrane

*I found it inescapably fascinating that the conception, composition, practice, and performance of a piece of music could blossom in a single moment, and come out whole and satisfying.... I had found a freedom that was both exhilarating and exacting*

—Stephen Nachmanovitch

*Play is the free spirit of exploration, doing and being for its own pure joy.*

—Stephen Nachmanovitch

On a Tuesday evening in late August 2001, Pulitzer Prize–winning trumpeter and composer Wynton Marsalis was playing at the Village Vanguard, one of the world's most famous jazz clubs. David Hajdu was there to see, hear, and relay the extraordinary moment.

Marsalis was playing a ballad, "I Don't Stand a Ghost of a Chance with You," unaccompanied. At the most dramatic point of his conclusion, someone's cell phone went off. Hajdu writes:

> Marsalis paused for a beat, motionless, and his eyebrows arched. I scrawled on a sheet of notepaper, MAGIC, RUINED. The cell-phone offender scooted into the hall as the chatter in the room grew louder. Still frozen at the microphone, Marsalis replayed the silly cell-phone melody note for note. Then he repeated it, and began improvising variations on the tune. The audience slowly came back to him. In a few minutes he resolved the improvisation—which had changed keys once or twice and throttled down to a ballad tempo—and ended up exactly where he had left off: "with … you … " The ovation was tremendous.[1]

Duke Ellington, who once said a problem is a chance for you to do your best, would have been proud.

## Improvisation and Jazz

Some, including most jazz artists, would say that Wynton Marsalis was simply being true to the spirit of jazz that night. While they would have, undoubtedly, marveled at the quality of his musical action, they would not have been totally surprised by the manner of his response. Improvisation, a jazz hallmark, derives from the Latin *im + provisus*, meaning "not provided" or "not foreseen." To play improvisationally is to play with trusting openness, to go wherever the music wants to go in the moment.

## WHY IMPROVISE?

### *(a literary improvisation)*

*Why improvise?*

*There is always more music to be heard and played than the music you have planned.*

*Why improvise?*

*To improvise is to create.*

*Why improvise?*

*To improvise is to be in search and to be surprised* ON PURPOSE.

*Why improvise?*

*Musicality is too, too rich not to.*

*Why improvise?*

*The Spirit says so.*

*Why improvise?*

*Improvisation is a way to be* F

R

E

E

!

David Hajdu's description of what happened that night is remarkable in the way that it highlights some essential elements of improvisation in general, and jazz improvisation in particular.

First, there is the *play* factor. Earlier in his article, prior to the moment of the ringing phone, Hajdu refers to Marsalis's *playing* of the final phrase: "I don't stand a ghost of a chance with you." To a large extent, the spirit of improvisation is the spirit of playfulness. I find Stephen Nachmanovitch's discussion of play in *Free Play: Improvisation in Life and Art* to be both insightful and energizing.

> In play we manifest fresh, interactive ways of relating with people, animals, things, ideas, images, ourselves.... We toss together elements that were formerly separate. Our actions take on novel sequences. To play is to free ourselves from arbitrary restrictions and expand our field of action. Our play fosters richness of response and adaptive flexibility. This is the evolutionary value of play—play makes us flexible. By reinterpreting reality and begetting novelty, we keep from becoming rigid. Play enables us to rearrange our capacities and our very identity so that we can be used in unforeseen ways.[2]

The integral connection between improvisation and play is in the bones of your memory. How much of your play was scripted as a child? The very essence of play was making things happen with the aid of playmates and play materials or toys. Everything was grist for play. The fun was in the making and the surprise, the appearance of new fulfillments that brought pleasure and expectation for the next discovery.

When the phone rang in the club that night, it caught Marsalis in the act of play. The phone became a toy, and although the embarrassed phone owner made a dash for the exit, he became for a moment Marsalis's surprise playmate. Marsalis received the phone's ringing into the arena of play that he already established. Marsalis heard the ringing, paused, as children often do when they play to sense and plot, and then he played with the ringing. It is important to note that when Marsalis paused, he didn't stop playing; he began to play at a different level, arguably a higher one. The pause was a part of the play. I believe the pause represented a zenith moment for his play. It was in the sterling moment of the pause that Marsalis imagined the creative potential of the ringing phone. The improvisational offering heard by the audience was played out by Marsalis in the pause as much as it was in the blowing of his trumpet.

Another key element in improvisation is *variation.* Marsalis began "improvising variations on the tune." The jazz artist operates under a great presumption. It is a presumption not shared by the masses. That presumption is that there are always a million and one ways—and more—to play something. Diversity and variety are accepted as being normative for creative expression. While many see creativity as a puddle that only a few step into, most jazz artists perceive creativity as something of a prodigious waterfall. They may not always be satisfied with the results of their creative pursuits, but their rightful need to pursue is taken for granted. Improvisation is the natural overflow of lavish creative expectation. Jazz artists seek to play many different sounds because they believe there are many different sounds to be played. Improvisation is a search for gems in a land the search party believes to be filled to running over with diamonds.

To believe that the depth of the riches is there is one thing, but to dare to go after the riches in the hopes that the discovery is more than worth it is another thing entirely. *Daring* is a third element of improvisation that you won't find without looking between the words in the account of what happened that night at the Village Vanguard. Daring is in the empty space between Marsalis beginning to play his variations and the audience "slowly coming back to him." Marsalis went out on a limb. He dared to believe that his creative risk would prove beneficial for all involved. Moreover, he dared to believe that even if he fell flat on his face, the musical journey into the wilderness of the unknown would still have been meaningful.

The element of daring is highlighted in the following seismic assessment by trumpeter Miles Davis of his musical expectations regarding *the* best-selling jazz recording in history, the largely improvised *Kind of Blue*:

> I wanted them to go beyond themselves. See, if you put a musician in a place where he has to do something different from what he does all the time, then he can do that—but he's got to think differently in order to do it. He has to use his imagination, be more creative, more innovative; he's got to take more risks. He's got to play above what he knows—far above it—and what that might lead to might take him above the place where he's been playing all along, to the new place where he finds himself right now—and to the next place he's going and even above that! . . . Because then anything can happen, and that's where great art and music happens [sic].[3]

Duke Ellington told his band members to play the notes as written, but "to keep some dirt in there somewhere," to be ready to play something they dared to play spontaneously, on-the-spot. Ellington himself served as a worthy model of jazz differentiation and variety. Noted jazz critic Stanley Crouch once observed, "Even when the personnel started to weaken in the late '60s as the demons of old age and death began to strip away his musicians, Ellington didn't stop creating. He seemed incapable of settling for an older version of himself."[4]

The final crucial element for quality improvisation, playing rich in its power to evoke as well as entertain, is *mastery*. Hajdu speaks of Marsalis "resolving the composition." What does he mean by that? Initially, his comment seems to run roughshod over the popular sentiment that improvisation is more a matter of surrender than it is control. Ellis Marsalis, Wynton's father, once said of improvisation that you really don't know where it's going to take you, and that you just let yourself go.

So how is it possible to let yourself go and "resolve the composition"? The answer is quality improvisation involves surrender and thought as well as intuitive forming and framing. Improvisation is spontaneity infused by preparation. Improvisational artistry is made possible by dedicated preparation prior to the moment of improvisation. Improvisational surrender happens on the backside of arduous preparation.

The best jazz improvisers draw from wells of notes, phrases, songs, and performances that they have played over and over again, alone and with others. Such practicing in the jazz world is called *shedding* or *wood-shedding*. Such arduous preparation creates a sense of musical fitness or "rightness." Marsalis's resolving the composition was his approaching the rightness established by his many hours of preparation.

Wynton Marsalis just happens to be one of the great *jazz shedders* of all time. Marsalis's creative club feat began years earlier when he was a teenager in New Orleans. His schedule included practicing his trumpet before school from 6:30 to 7 A.M., after lunch from 12:30 to 1 P.M., at school from 2:30 to 3 P.M., and after school from 6 to 6:30 P.M. Marsalis practiced for no fewer than two hours a day. His practice hours increased as he grew older, as did his emotional and professional commitment to his craft. Marsalis told an interviewer once: "One thing about excellence, it's an exclusive club. And it's only for those who really want to pay dues."[5]

The best improvisation happens on the backside of practice. Serious musical practitioners create for themselves an ever-expanding well of musical options. The chances for them to improvise well greatly increases with the discovery and mastery of new musical options. In addition to developing a well of creative options, practice breeds familiarity with the instrument, its ability and its potential. The more time spent with the instrument, the more trust the musician is able to place into it. Finally, there is the instrument of the musician herself. Practice breeds personal daring and, ultimately, mastery. One dares more readily having dared and lived a hundred thousand times before.

## Improvisation and Preaching

One way to address the matter of improvisation and preaching is to focus on the four features of improvisation we have just identified: *play*, *variety*, *daring*, and *mastery*.

### *Play*

Some might have a negative visceral reaction to the idea of preaching as play. This may have something to do with the fact that most of us generally associate religion with solemnity. God is to be feared, not played with. To connect preaching with play, we may first have to begin thinking about God in ways that transcend seriousness. One effective way to do this is to walk around the places where our faith makes us smile and laugh, or dare to discover such places.

The Scripture is very funny to me in places. For instance, the story of Sarah and Abraham in Genesis 18:9-15. Sarah laughs because she overhears a surprise dinner guest say something really, really funny. He assures ninety-year-old Sarah and one-hundred-year-old Abraham that they are going to be the proud parents of a bouncing baby boy. Sarah shakes her head and laughs to herself. And she thinks, "I can see it now, me at my age pushing a baby stroller up Main Street. A baby at ninety, I can just hear myself calling out to Abraham: 'Abe, while you're out, don't forget to pick up some diapers!' This guy, whoever he is, has had a little too much grape juice." Maybe he has: but Sarah soon discovers, whatever the stranger's emotional state, he can still hear pretty well. He heard Sarah's private (not-so-private) laughter and calls her on it. She, perhaps embarrassed at getting caught, denies that she laughed. In my version of how it went, Sarah and the stranger then go back and forth like children on a playground: "You laughed," says the stranger. "Did not," Sarah responds. "Did too." "Did not." The stranger walks off into the distance, leaving Sarah standing with the comforting accomplishment of having had the last word. But before he is completely out of sight, he suddenly turns and yells back, "Did too!" The stranger is dead set on having Sarah own her laughter.

There are recurring themes in Scripture that make me smile. One of them is the lunacy of grace. There is no rhyme or reason to the grace of God. It will show up whenever and wherever, and anyone is liable to get it on him or her. In *Telling the Truth*, Frederick Buechner captures the lunacy of grace when he describes Zacchaeus as the man who climbs up a sycamore tree a crook and climbs down a saint, and Paul as the man who sets out as a hatchet man for the Pharisees and comes back a fool for Christ.

I smile when I observe and think about the sheer vastness of the universe and the outlandish diversity of it all. And the joke is on us. Just when the experts think they have one mystery solved, another one breaks out. For example, in recent years astronomers have been walloped by the discovery of new planets, and evidence that the universe, as vast as it is, appears to be expanding. This sort of thing gives fresh meaning to the line in the song "Great Is Thy Faithfulness": "Morning by morning, new mercies I see."

When it comes to humor, joke of jokes, the laughter trail leads to God. Does God's creative range exclude the reality of laughter? If God made it all, *all* necessarily includes laughter. What would it mean for you to interpret God's reality in a lighter light, to believe that God moves not only in mysterious ways but often in very sneaky, subversive, and amusing ways? What if Dario Fo is right? Fo is one of Italy's great playwrights and clowns. He won the 1997 Nobel Prize for literature. When he was first informed of this, he thought it was a big joke. Assured and reassured that it was not, Fo exclaimed, "God is a clown!"

Finally, there are some curious etymological linkages between divinity and playfulness. John Ayto's *Dictionary of Word Origins* includes the following entry on *play*:

> The origins of play are obscure. It had a relative in Middle Dutch *pleien* "dance about, jump for joy," but this has now died out, leaving it in splendid but puzzling isolation, its ancestry unaccounted for.[6]

And there is this: *lila* is an old Sanskrit word that means "divine play, the creative, destructive, and re-creative play of God." Amazingly enough, *lila* also means "love."

Daring to imagine a playful God can free you to responsibly cultivate playfulness in preaching. Indeed, you may find that in the flow of a religious life that receives laughter more freely, you won't be able to help yourself. Pianist Vicki Vogel Schmidt calls her creative work "Spirit Play."

### *Variety (Having More Than Enough to Say)*

The critical key to quality improvising in preaching is being a sponge in life. Be awake and aware as a way of life. Practice keen attentiveness as much as possible. Sermon material is everywhere: conversations, books, experiences, pains, reflections, surprises, and anything else you can name. The kind of attentiveness I am referring to is hot at two levels. You want to pay attention to life first for life's sake, and second for sermonizing's sake. The goal is to be constantly taking in, consciously and unconsciously, the great wealth of human existence. You can aid the process by journaling regularly and keeping notebooks for sightings, hearings, and feelings along the way. You want to preach from a full well. When the well is full, items more easily surface to the mind for instant articulation during the moment of preaching. We say not because we have not.

How do you fill your mental well, so much so that there is more information ready to come to the fore spontaneously during the preaching act? Take responsibility for filling the well.

Cultivate a curious disposition. Be curious as a way of life, or as poet Stanley Kunitz encourages, "be explorers all your life." It is amazing how much material, including potential improvisational additions, can be accumulated from just asking questions. Several years ago when I began my seminary teaching career, I was always afraid of not having enough material to fill a three-hour class. It wasn't long before I realized that the key to having enough to say was related to questions—the ones I asked in my preparation, and the ones I asked along with my students in class.

Questions are the great generators of intellectual search and acquisition. A searching mind will never be at a loss when it comes to having something to say. When all else fails, you simply say the questions. Questions can sustain and stimulate conversation better than anything. Speaking of questions, don't be afraid to ask them aloud during the preaching event. It is one of the most effective ways of keeping a congregation awake and engaged during the sermon. Rainer Marie Rilke's admonition is golden: "Love the questions themselves."

Another way to fill your preaching well is to pay attention to the *shavings*. When it's been a good sermon-preparation week you will have almost as much material left over (shavings on the floor) as you have material that you plan to preach. In my experience, those that did not make it into my final preaching draft have a way of sneaking into the pulpit as thoughts and inspirations during the preaching event. Being sensitive to such intrusions can make for great improvisational enhancements in preaching.

Though shavings on the floor, these are thoughts that have already been filtered through the critical faculties of your mind. When they arrive as you are preaching, you have the luxury of knowing that they rightfully relate to the sermon in some way. Because of this prior familiarity, you can more freely grant them admission into a sermon already in progress. You can facilitate openness to shavings by keeping a file of all materials and work on any given sermon. After you have finished your final draft, simply review material in your folder. Your goal is to keep these things in your unconscious mind. While you have previously determined that they will not fit the planned preaching event, your mood, the moment, the congregation, and the Spirit may inspire otherwise during the preaching event. As I am writing this, the image of football players sitting on the sideline bench comes to mind. Many of the players dressed for a football game do not play. They are part of the second or third teams, called on to substitute for another player if the game demands such. Think of preaching improvisations as second and third preaching material that you may call on to play if the moment demands such. Improvisational preaching is the inflow and overflow of your preparation.

### *Daring*

Saxophonist Sonny Rollins is known for his expansive improvisational solos. He has been referred to as a "spontaneous orchestrator." Here's how he describes his experience with improvisation:

> Whenever I try to create solos when I'm playing, what I am basically trying to do is blot out my mind as much as possible. Of course, I have already learned the material. After learning the material I try to blot out my mind and let it flow by itself. So I try not to really think too much about what I am playing when I am playing. I sort of have the structure already and then I try to create and let it come by itself.[7]

There is a whole lot of daring involved in preaching. To stand up and speak on behalf of God is one of the greatest risks of all. But the *call risk* to preach is fodder for another conversation. When it comes to preaching and improvisation, the risk is to mentally abandon all prior preparation, to let it go, to surrender it. This is surrender on the backside of prior preparation, but surrender nonetheless. The surrender makes a place, a space, for improvisation to happen. This is risky, threatening business; all voids are. But unless you are willing to yield the space, you will not be able to experience the filling of it with fresh communicative meaning.

To facilitate the release of preparation, on Sunday mornings just before preaching, I sometimes imagine myself releasing a bird into the air. This is my way of ritualizing the emptying-to-be-filled process. I risk surrendering all I studied in preparation for the sermon in the hope that it will soar away somewhere, fill itself with fresh water, and fly back to me in the preaching moment. Sometimes the bird looks and feels very similar to how it did before it flew away. Sometimes the bird looks and feels like a different bird entirely.

Emptying is a form of hospitality. It sends a sign of welcome to the spirit of improvisation. Moreover it signals your cognitive and intuitive self to be alert for fresh thoughts, connections, and communicative devices while preaching. Emptying is a spiritual and intellectual primer for improvisation.

My experience with emptying is that it also serves to relax me before preaching. Once, while watching a televised track and field event, I heard the announcer say of one sprinter, "All he needs to do now is let the race come out." The commentator was referring to the fact that the sprinter had trained sufficiently and now, more than anything else, needed to relax within his training. Not being able to relax could send stressors running through his body, tightening him up, and in effect sabotaging his rigorous preparation for the race.

I have never read a paragraph on preaching tightness, but one is in order. Too many preachers, and not just novices, are too tight. The busyness of the week, insufficient preparation, and muted confidence are just three of the things that can suppress the preaching spirit. When we are too tight not only is spontaneity blocked, but even what we planned to say has a way of coming out all wrong, or not coming out at all. All the more reason for preachers to create their own pre-sermon emptying rituals. Preachers have to discover ways to let the preaching come out in all of its planned and improvisational sound and faith. When done effectively, such emptying cultivates what I believe to be the preferred pre-sermon mood: a state of relaxed confidence.

## *Mastery*

Everyone can improvise. Only persons who are willing to commit to their craft are able to improvise at levels that cause others to notice with deep satisfaction and appreciation. Ideally, the best soil for sermon improvisation is gross absorption and familiarity. Mastery in any field is a key that unlocks the door to deeper knowledge and ability.

Impotency and hesitancy may get in the way of our embracing mastery in preaching. I need to tread delicately here. In our faith tradition we tend to trumpet human frailty and humility both, inarguable facts of life to be sure. Playing such notes too long, however, can keep one from leaning into the greatness and energy of humanness anointed by God. Our tradition is not without those themes, either. Thus we may be free and inspired to pursue living and preaching mastery, the latter being an ever-expanding creative excellence in preaching.

As preachers, we are challenged to be filled with power without being full of ourselves, and to preach deliberately without being closed-minded and dismissive of others. This is servant-mastery. When such mastery is experienced, greatness can happen. Once, while speaking to a large crowed of people in a public worship service, a preacher began to improvise his message in the middle of his planned address. He began to say things he'd thought and said before but hadn't thought to say that day. The people and moment called it out of him. The preacher was Martin Luther King, Jr., and that public worship service was the March on Washington, August 28, 1963. King's legendary "I Have a Dream" oration was an improvisation for the ages. Michael Eric Dyson suggests that King's preaching/speaking in general was filled with elements of jazz:

> King spoke much the way a jazz musician plays, improvising from minimally or maximally sketched chords or fingering changes that derive from hours of practice and performance. The same song is never the same song, and for King, the same speech was certainly never the same speech. He constantly added and subtracted, attaching a phrase here and paring a paragraph there to suit the situation. He could bend ideas and slide memorized passages through his trumpet of a voice with remarkable sensitivity to his audience's make-up.[8]

Finally, preaching mastery cannot happen without spiritual infusion. In the black church, spontaneous speechmaking is inextricably linked with Holy Spirit presence. It's important to know what you are going to say, but it's even more important "to let the Spirit use you." Not only does the Spirit know what needs to be said in the moment, but the Spirit knows how it needs to be said and to whom it needs to be said. The Spirit is the Sacred Improvisational Helper, prompting the preacher with unrehearsed sounds and hushes. Yes, hushes. Do not discount the importance of surprise silence, the unplanned preaching pause. Too often we say too much too fast, and don't provide sufficient space for people to ponder substantive pronouncements. We need the Spirit to help us discern and practice the grace and pace of great preaching. We need the Spirit to make the sermon sing and dance in the open spaces and tight corners of preaching. The African American church tradition has always believed that there were far too many factors involved in such communication for pulpit and pew to effectively command them all by themselves. The Spirit needed to be "in the midst." The Spirit needed to "stop by." Now, more than thirty years into my preaching adventure, I concur without coercion: *To preach finely and fully in any sermonic moment, we need divine anointing and blessing.*

Remember when all is said and done, it's not about preaching first, it's about living. James Forbes reminds us in his book *The Holy Spirit and Preaching*: "Because of the anointing, Jesus preached with power. He preached not only with words, but his life was the 'amen' to the proclamation of his lips."[9]

Barbara Brown Taylor's disclaimer about the Sunday morning sermon is right on:

> There is more going on than anyone can say. Preaching is finally more than art or science. It is alchemy, in which tin becomes gold and yard rocks become diamonds under the influence of the Holy Spirit.[10]

## Exercises and Resources

1. Read and take notes on *Free Play: Improvisation in Life and Art*, by Stephen Nachmanovitch.

2. Read and take notes on chapter 4, "The Life of Study," in Fred Craddock's *Preaching* (Abingdon Press, 1985).

3. Verbally and silently practice improvisation. Work on saying various portions of your sermon in different ways. Fall in love with the idea, but experiment with multiple modes of communicative transportation.

4. Leave spaces for improvisation in your manuscript or notes. Go to the pulpit prepared to freshly word what you will say in places.

5. In your improvisation practice and preaching, focus on patience, on giving yourself time to conceptualize and articulate the new thing inside of you. Practice paying attention in the pauses between the words. Often the difference between a good word and the best word is just a couple of seconds.

6. Hold a postsermon debriefing session. No more than a few hours after your sermon, take a few moments to review the presentation in your mind, or better yet listen to a tape. Note the places where you improvised. The debriefing session should include at least three components:

(a) *Analysis:* Examine the nature of your improvisation. Did you add something? Did you refine something? Did you say something in a different way? Did you delete something? Did the improvisation occur in the on-the-spot rearrangement of material? Note what you did.

(b) *Excavation:* Dig up and out what it was that inspired you to improvise. Did a thought left in the study sneak into the pulpit? Were you stimulated by a facial expression in the congregation? What sparked the fire of improvisation?

(c) *Evaluation:* Determine the overall worth of the improvisation(s) to your sermon. In what ways did your improvisation improve and/or detract from the sermon?

A few months of debriefing in this way will cultivate an improvisational consciousness, competency, and confidence that may even have accomplished jazz musicians nodding their heads in approval.

## Notes

1. David Hajdu, "Wynton's Blues," *The Atlantic Monthly* (March 2003), 44.

2. Nachmanovitch, *Free Play*, 43.

3. Spencer, "Miles Davis's *Kind of Blue*," *Theology Today* (January 1996), 508.

4. Stanley Crouch, "Duke Ellington: Jazz Artist of the Century," *JazzTimes* (December 1999).

5. Touré, "Wynton Marsalis," *Icon Thoughtstyle Magazine*.

6. John Ayto, *Dictionary of Word Origins* (New York: Arcade, 1990), 398.

7. From the Robert Mugge film *Sonny Rollins: Saxophone Colossus* (Winstar, 1986).

8. Michael Eric Dyson, *I May Not Get There with You: The True Martin Luther King, Jr.* (New York: The Free Press, 2000), 143.

9. James Forbes, *The Holy Spirit and Preaching* (Nashville: Abingdon Press, 1989), 43.

10. Barbara Brown Taylor, *The Preaching Life* (Cambridge, MA: Cowley Publications, 1993), 85.

CHAPTER SIX

# Can I Get a Witness? Dialogue in Jazz and Preaching

*I get a sense of accomplishment when I connect with the audience—the looks, the applause, the remarks—it's like the flowing of a river that never stops.*

—Leon Merian, jazz trumpeter

*If everyone is in a frisky spirit, the spirit gets to me and I can make my trombone sing.*

—Jim Robinson, jazz trombonist

## The Church's Gift to Jazz

In the preceding chapters we began with jazz. This chapter begins with church and preaching because the dialogical reality of jazz was inspired in part by the call and response of black church worship. Throughout our conversation the emphasis has been on how jazz *may* inform preaching for the better. Through *call and response* the church *did* influence jazz for the better. Call and response is the church's inspired, if unintended, magnificent contribution to jazz:

> *Call* and *response* refers to the Sunday service: "Say 'Amen' somebody"—"AMEN!" This interaction between preachers and congregations all over black America has become an integral feature of cultural expression in the United States. Born in West and Central Africa, where one experiences it in exchanges among singers and instrumentalists (as well as dancers and sculptors), in the U.S. this pattern occurs in church songs and sermons and also in work songs, play songs (such as "Little Sally Walker"), blues, rags, and in jazz. You say something; I say something back.[1]

Beneath the dialogical impulse of worship and jazz is a dialogical understanding of life. Living happens in relationship with others. This is the juicy fruit of the West African–rooted communal sense of self in which personhood is rightfully manifested in group relationships. Community and personhood are understood to be both sides of the same coin.

In the church, the dialogue is usually between congregation and the worship leader at the time—the preacher, prayer, or singer. Usually the congregation is urging the worship leader on: "PREACH it!" "SAY your prayers." "You BETTER sing!" But I have found out through experience and research that more than encouragement is at work when the church talks together. Having preached in the dialogical black church tradition since my early teens, I have always been fascinated with call and response, not to mention dependent on it. I grew up having people help me preach with their verbal admonitions.

When I was considering a subject for my doctor of ministry program at Emory University's Candler School of Theology, I seized the opportunity to learn more about the dynamic dialogical dimension of preaching. Beacon Light Baptist Church, my first senior pastorate, joined me in investigating this religious hallmark. Through surveys, listening sessions, and discussions, we discovered three main features of the traditional talk-back between people and preacher: (1) dialogue builds community; (2) dialogue helps the preacher gauge her or his effectiveness in communication; and (3) dialogue helps the listener understand the message. Here are a few of the written responses to a question about the perceived meaning and value of dialogue:

- opens my mind and heart to a better understanding of God's word
- gets me more involved in worship
- gives me a sense of personal communication with the pastor
- makes the atmosphere more comfortable when the pastor receives more input from the congregation
- gives a feeling of unity
- it lets me know that the Spirit is alive
- it helps me to respond, encourage, and witness
- we feel and react as one; it creates a bond between us and God
- positive dialogue stimulates growth
- the pastor knows that you are listening
- the pastor learns about what educational and emotional level he or she needs to work from
- it is a way of expressing the personality of the church

As experienced by the members of Beacon Light Baptist Church, it is hard to imagine sermonizing with the dialogue turned off. At the core of call and response is a way of actively being with self, community, and mystery. Dialogue is the sacred conversation with life.

## The Dialogue of Jazz

At this moment I am listening to "The Single Petal of a Rose," a soft slow Ellington classic, being played by Greg Osby (alto saxophone), Nicholas Payton (trumpet), Harold O'Neil (piano), Robert Hurst (bass), and Rodney Green (drums). Osby and Payton are taking turns playing the melody. Throughout, O'Neil, Hurst, and Green are providing underlying cushion, or background accompaniment, improvising in stellar supportive ways. O'Neil has just taken the melody. He is playing with delicate touch and precise dexterity. The horns are silent. Hurst is playing long and deliberate notes on the bass. Green is holding a conversation between the cymbals and the drums within the larger musical conversation. The horns are back. Payton and Osby are talking to each other. One calls, the other responds; sometimes they end up on the same note. The pleasant conversation just concluded.

In jazz, the dialogue can be between instruments and musicians, or between the pianist's left hand and the right. It may be between a singer, an instrument, and a song. The dialogue can happen between a bandleader and a band, and between a band and an audience. In jazz there are always multiple dialogues happening at the same time. Jazz music is a communal concoction of the highest and deepest order. The credo of jazz dialogue is this: *We are all responsible for and to the music*.

Jazz dialogue is about teasing and taunting, and prodding and pushing each other to new musical places. Sometimes the pushing turns into shoving:

> They [call and response musical conversations] may also involve knock-down competitions, challenges, games of innuendo, ritual insult, mockery. Sometimes signifying contests (also called "cutting contests") involve big-mouthing and virtuoso sounding off.[2]

The cutting was a part of the communal search for new musical sounds.

Such dialogue facilitates a sense of social accountability. You are never just playing for yourself. You are playing with and for your musical partners, and for those who have gone and those yet to come. When you honor the craft and the tradition by offering unique excellence, the accomplishment gets noticed by the guild if not the masses. Art Tatum is regarded by many as the greatest jazz pianist of them all. He once told Oscar Peterson, whom many believe to be the second greatest jazz pianist ever, "Listen, there's an old man in Kansas City. He knows only one chorus of the blues. The man can't play the second chorus. And every time I'm there I go to hear him because nobody plays the blues like him. Everyone has something to say in music—if he has *some* talent and has the discipline to master even one chorus."[3]

People, places, and things are a part of the dialogue of jazz. The inspiration for "Freddie Freeloader," my favorite song on the *Kind of Blue* album, was a smart, lively person of the streets who worked as a bartender and who hung around jazz musicians and survived on handouts. The person's business card acknowledged his lifestyle as a freeloader.

In *Duke Ellington: A Spiritual Biography*, Jana Tull Steed recounts Duke Ellington being mentored in the matter of paying attention to life:

> From Bubber Miley, especially, Duke learned the importance of paying attention to what was around him. Bubber showed him a way of translating sights into sound. The trumpet player would take his inspiration from an advertising sign, a name, an overheard phrase. He'd say the syllables slowly. He'd play around with pitch, inflection, and phrasing. Then Bubber would take up his horn and translate these sounds into riffs that imitated the rise and fall and cadence of the human voice.[4]

Decades later when Wynton Marsalis played "the phone notes" that night at the Village Vanguard, he was "witnessing" in the waters of a great heritage of attentiveness and inventiveness. He was doing more than blowing his horn; he was trumpeting, in zenith register, the dialogical musical tradition that is jazz.

## The Dialogue of Preaching

At first glance it would appear that there are four dialogical partners in preaching: the Spirit, the Bible, the preacher, and the congregation. Members of my Jazz of Preaching class yielded the following expanded list of frequent dialogical partners:

| | |
|---|---|
| God | Tradition |
| Jesus | Scholarship |
| Holy Spirit | Symbols |
| Bible | The Topic |
| Preacher | The Lectionary |

| | |
|---|---|
| Congregation | Beliefs |
| Choir | Values |
| Current Events | Surprises |
| Musicians | The Public-at-Large |
| Children | Distractions |
| Silence | The Weather |
| The Week | The Mood |
| Prayers | Stories |
| Space | Disappointments |
| Light | Celebrations |
| Sounds | Hopes |
| Scents | Fears |

Though we may condense the list with categorizations, it would still be a formidable list. Survey the list. Which items would you identify as primary and secondary dialogical partners? Which partners do you pay most attention to? With which partners do you wish to establish a greater dialogue? What's missing from the list?

Two behaviors are essential for preachers to preach effectively amidst such a vast array of frequent and infrequent influences: *listening up* and *speaking up*.

I discussed listening in an earlier chapter. But too much cannot be said about it. These days the great threat to listening is hurry. I write about this malady in my book

*Addicted to Hurry: Spiritual Strategies for Slowing Down* (Judson Press, 2003). We take so little time to listen carefully to the sounds and the silences because we are constantly on the go. We barely hear even the ones who are closest to us. The cost of our inattentiveness is foggy living. And we get used to the fog. We lose our appetites for the rich delicacies of clarity and depth.

Writer Gina Greenlee says, "I think hyperbusyness is the cocaine of the 21st century." Such an addiction cuts to the core of the preaching enterprise. Poet Carolyn Forché laments, "The velocity of human experience has so accelerated that perhaps our capacity to sustain contemplation is being eroded." Where there is no time for contemplation, there can be no real preaching. Slowing down and paying attention is the great challenge of our time. It is a revolutionary act in a warp-speed world. Rebellion is the only option for the real preacher. *Slow down and listen in life, in sermon preparation, and in the pulpit.*

What about speaking up? Here, I mean something more than the action of verbalizing words. One morning our daughter, Joya, sat at the computer typing away. When I asked what she was working on, she replied, "A speech." I smiled. Speech was one of my favorite classes in high school. I enjoyed preparing for and participating in oratorical contests around Louisiana. Two of my favorite teachers throughout my high school years were Mrs. Brown and Miss Perry, my speech teachers. As I prepared my coffee, I reminisced, and then said to Joya: "Oh yes, speech. Do you want to know the secrets of speech making?" When I asked the question, I had no idea what I was going to answer. I was just basking in the moment of fond remembrance. My question was the overflow of affection. I didn't have a clue about what I was going to propose as the secrets of speech making. Finally, when Joya asked me to share my revelations, I paused a moment, and then said, "Well, the first secret is . . . CONFIDENCE." I heard myself think the word; I couldn't stop myself from saying the word. In the immediate pause after the pronouncement, I felt no impulse to take back what I'd said. Indeed, I went even further. "Joya, do you want to know what the second secret of speech making is? CONFIDENCE."

I won't take it back in terms of preaching, either. Having faithful trust in yourself, your calling, your sermon, and the Holy Spirit is a crucial requirement for quality dialogue. I suspect that confidence deprivation is at the root of much unconvincing preaching. Lack of confidence can sabotage a well-prepared sermon by a reasonably articulate preacher. It is revealing that the one problem God knew he had to fix for Moses was Moses' confidence problem. His checkered background and stuttering were nonissues when it came to fulfilling the mandate to bring God's message of deliverance. From burning bush to divine definitive identification ("I AM THAT I AM"), God was focused on instilling within Moses the confidence to play his part, not without fear, but in spite of it and through it.

With confidence we can freely play our part in the jazz of preaching. It is a part that no one else in all the world can play. It is a part that God, creation, church, and community are counting on us to play, even as they play their parts. It is a part that cannot be done in by mistakes because mistakes become invitations for new discovery in jazz. There are no wrong notes for long. Maybe there are no wrong notes at all. With all such assurances, confidence is still not inevitable. Confidence is a choice, one that we are called to make over and over again. We are challenged to, as one writer says of her craft, lean into our sound and sensibility. When such strength is absent, always remember that there is a strength beyond our strength.

Robert K. Cooper's *The Other 90%: How to Unlock Your Vast Untapped Potential for Leadership and Life* is filled with memorable insights from Cooper's grandfathers. One of them was a physician who continued to see patients even as he suffered with pancreatic cancer. Toward the end of his life, he was called in to operate on a young accident victim. The child was near death and there was no other surgeon nearby skilled enough to perform the delicate procedure. Nurses and attending physicians recall a remarkable transition, or perhaps a better word for it is *transcendence*, that day. The physician stood at the edge of the operating table sweating and trembling. Then he took a deep breath, got himself together, and began to perform the surgery. His hands were steady, not shaking at all during the surgery. The child survived.

Persons present may have wondered how a dying doctor could draw forth such amazing strength. His grandson did not have to wonder; he knew. His grandfather had told him that before every surgery he would pause outside the operating room and offer up a silent prayer that confessed weakness before the mysteries of life and ultimate powers of healing, but ended with these words: "Call upon the best in me."[5]

This is not a bad presermon-confidence-building prayer. Not bad at all.

## Exercises and Resources

1. Interview a jazz musician. Talk with her or him about the experience of playing with others.

2. Listen to a jazz album. Note how the dialogue is happening. What are the characteristic features of the dialogue? Some listening suggestions:

*The Complete Ella Fitzgerald and Louis Armstrong*

*Kind of Blue*, Miles Davis

*Time Out*, The Dave Brubeck Quartet

*The Classic Quartet*, John Coltrane

3. Identify five ways in which the congregation informs your preaching verbally and/or nonverbally on any given Sunday.
4. Develop five ways to enhance dialogue with your congregation?
5. What are your most important dialogical partners in preaching? Why?
6. What are your least favorite dialogical partners? Why?
7. Meet with area preachers and congregants to work on a sermon together. Evaluate your experience and compare it to working on a sermon alone.
8. Read or reread Martin Buber's *I and Thou* (Free Press, 1971).

NOTES

1. Robert O'Meally, "Call and Response," *Seeing Jazz: Artists and Writers on Jazz* (San Francisco: Chronicle Books, 1997), 85.
2. Ibid.
3. Oscar Peterson, *The Will to Swing* (New York: Cooper Square Press, 2000), 102.
4. Jana Tull Steed, *Duke Ellington: A Spiritual Biography* (New York: Crossroad, 1999), 49.
5. Robert K. Cooper, *The Other 90%: How to Unlock Your Vast Untapped Potential for Leadership and Life* (New York: Three Rivers Press, 2001), 272.

CHAPTER SEVEN

# Blues Preaching

*There is a meaning beyond absurdity.*
—Abraham Heschel

*The contradictions of life are not final.*
—Howard Thurman

*[Count] Basie never stopped crying. He sat there and wept. He never stopped crying.*
—Attendee at Duke Ellington's funeral

*Our ability to grow is directly proportional to an ability to entertain the uncomfortable.*
—Twyla Tharp, choreographer

To play and sing the blues is to sing woundedness. This is not always a sad performance. For after all, one is still playing and singing; one is yet alive with the bitter and the sweet through it all. In *The Spirituals and the Blues*, James Cone defines the blues "as a state of mind in relation to the truth of black experience."

Furthermore, Cone offers the following definitive features of the blues:

1. The blues reflect on the incongruity of life and attempt to make meaning in a situation filled with contradictions.

2. The blues is an encounter with through melody and rhythm.

3. The blues express strength in brokenness.

4. The blues affirm the essential value of black humanity.

5. The blues focus on everyday life.[1]

Preaching, especially pastoral preaching, involves wording woundedness. We do not pastor long before we are called on to preach to and through trouble. The blues tradition is a formidable reservoir of instruction for preaching in the valley. I believe three artists in particular have the most to offer preachers on the subject of blues preaching. Allow me to introduce professors Holiday, Scott, and Coltrane.

## Billie Holiday and Honesty

I dreamed once that I was in a setting where racism was being discussed. In the dream I was increasingly troubled by the level of the discussion. We were not dealing with the matters at any depth. After a while we entered a time of intermission. Suddenly, we were all gathered in the room again, but before anyone could speak, a woman, while still seated, began to sing. She was singing a Billie Holiday song, though I do not remember which one. The song transformed the mood. Suddenly it was my turn to speak. I began by saying that I felt the song had set a more promising tone for genuine discourse.

Several notable Billie Holiday fans point to her musical honesty:

> She sang every song . . . as if she had written it that very morning.[2]
>
> —Maya Angelou

> Nobody—I mean nobody—was more honest than Billie Holiday![3]
>
> —Tony Bennett

Jazz vocal stylist Cassandra Wilson connects Holiday's honesty to her tone: "Billie's tone was so unique, and transcendent."[4]

I am listening to Billie Holiday this very moment. She is singing a song called "Gloomy Sunday." The recording was just released in 2001. It is a slow, plodding song that begins in grief. A loved one has died, and leaving has left the mourner with the deepest gloom.

There is a brief musical interlude and then Holiday sings a stanza, comparable in length to the first, that announces a decision to "end it all."

What happens next has to be one of the great transitions in musical history. The song suddenly turns on the wings of Holiday's voice, deliberately but ever so smoothly, saying that she was only dreaming:

> I wake and I find you
> asleep in the deep of my heart, dear.

The magic of the song is that you never see the turn until it's time. Holiday is so true to the grief lyrics in the beginning of the song that she brings you to the graveyard. When she transitions, there is a jolt. Not only was she dreaming, but you were as well, and now you are swimming in the cool refreshing waters of emotional relief, fully awake. The song works because Holiday gives full voice to the song—its agony and its ascent.

Blues preaching gives full voice to the painful places of life. It is as honest about sorrow as it is about joy. In this regard, Billie Holiday sings in the lament tradition of biblical faith. In lament, sorrow is not washed away before it is acknowledged as sorrow. Lament is not afraid to look at the blood and the dirt, and name it for what it is. The opposite of blues preaching is sterilized preaching, preaching cleansed of the paradoxes and punishments of life. True gospel preaching is blues preaching. It finds ways to honor the hurt without romanticizing it. It knows that the only way for glorious Sunday to have any merit is to have it stand and face gloomy Sunday without shrinking. Blues preaching is glory *through* gloom.

## John Coltrane and Perseverance

John Coltrane's *A Love Supreme*, a jazz staple, is a four-part journey of faith: "Acknowledgement," "Resolution," "Pursuance," and "Psalm." The suite was recorded in one evening with supreme musicians: pianist McCoy Tyner, bassist Jimmy Garrison, and drummer Elvin Jones. *A Love Supreme* is the amalgam of an artist who had practiced a religious devotion to his instrument from his youth, had wrestled with the demon of chemical addiction, and had found peace with God. Mastery + Suffering + God =

Dynamite. Through his horn Coltrane blew his way home. Listen to *A Love Supreme* and you can almost see his soul reaching, searching, and finding. No screeches ever sounded so sacred. U2's lead singer, Bono, offers the following tribute that names the dearth of an alleged spiritual well, and the surprising abundance of a new inspirational source:

> I was at the top of the Grand Hotel in Chicago [on tour in 1987] listening to *A Love Supreme* and learning the lesson of a lifetime. Earlier I had been watching televangelists remake God in their own image: tiny, petty, and greedy. Religion has become the enemy of God, I was thinking...religion was what happened when God, like Elvis, has left the building. I knew from my earliest memories that the world was winding in a direction away from love and I too was caught in its drag. There is so much wickedness in this world but beauty is our consolation prize ... the beauty of John Coltrane's reedy voice, its whispers, its knowingness, its sly sexuality, its praise of creation. And so Coltrane began to make sense to me. I left the music on repeat and I stayed awake listening to a man facing God with the gift of his music.[5]

For his part, Coltrane testified:

> My goal is to live the truly religious life and express it in my music. If you live it, when you play there's no problem because the music is just part of the whole thing. To be a musician is really something. It goes very, very deep. My music is the spiritual expression of what I am—my faith, my knowledge, my being.... I'd like to point out to people the divine in a musical language that transcends words. I want to speak to their souls.[6]

From time to time in the Jazz of Preaching classes we imagine the great jazz musicians playing for and addressing a gathering of preachers. I imagine Coltrane playing *A Love Supreme*. After he is done, there is an extended pause. When Coltrane speaks, he doesn't make statements, he asks questions.

*Who is God to you?*

*How did God call you?*

*Where does it hurt?*

*How do you play pain in your preaching?*

*How does the Spirit move you?*

*How do you pray?*

*How do you pray when you don't have the words?*

Our answers give away the tenor of our spiritual striving—and, hopefully, resting. Our answers say something about the stuff under our preaching, the matters of deepening commitment through it all. Our spiritual perseverance is what gives preaching its integrity and resonating spiritual tonality. When such a tone is heard, people know that it is genuine because it touches their reality—and longing.

## Jimmy Scott and Patience

When I first heard Jimmy Scott sing I could not believe my ears. He sang "When Did You Leave Heaven." When he was through, I thought he was the one who'd skipped out of heaven. The evidence was his voice.

Jimmy Scott's unique high voice is a result of Kallmann's syndrome, which prevented him from experiencing the natural physiological changes of adolescence. Scott took his affliction and turned it into a gift.

> I might have been teased and tortured, but I grew to see my affliction as my gift. When I sang, I soared. I could soar higher than all those hurts aimed at my heart. . . . I saw my suffering as my salvation. Once I knew that, I understood God had put me in this strange little package for a reason. All I needed was the courage to be me. That courage took a lifetime to develop.[7]

The first thing I noticed about Scott's heavenly singing was his voice. The second thing that I noticed was his pace. He sang slow, more slowly than anyone I had ever heard before. I was even more keenly aware of it because at the time I was trying to slow my life down. What I later learned was Scott's signature style became a living example of living life at a slower, *savoring pace*. Jimmy Scott savors every note. His biographer, David Ritz, writes in *Faith in Time*:

> He does more than take his time. He doesn't worry about time. Time disappears as a restraint or measure. As a singer, his signatures are idiosyncratic phrasing and radical, behind-the-beat syncopation.[8]

Scott explains his style as follows:

> If you believe in the beat, you don't need to worry about the beat. It's there. Always been there and always will. You don't have to follow it. Fact is, the beat sets you free. It's your security, your heartbeat, an expression of God, a gift. Time is a gift. Time is our life. I believe in time just like I believe in God. All that gives me faith in time. If we're in the moment, if we're truly rooted in what we're doing when we're doing it, we can work through all the bad stuff. In that sense, we can all be singers singing away our sadness.[9]

Jimmy Scott's musical patience stands in stark contrast to the kind of fast-paced preaching prevalent in many pulpits. Our hurry is fueled by a speed-addicted culture and church members who believe a church service ought to conclude at an unchangeable time. There may be other reasons for homiletical hurry, including careless preparation, a lack of gravity about what it is that we are doing, and an overall lack of confidence in our ability to hold a congregation's attention with an old story for any extended length of time. So, many preachers hurry in and hurry out with as little harm done as possible.

Jimmy Scott challenges preachers to be more patient in their sermonizing, especially in the tender places (eulogies, for example), where sermons ought to leave spaces to account for wounded hearts and slowed spirits. Patient preaching is preaching that understands the value of pauses and waiting. Patient preaching knows that it's not just what you say but how you say it that can make a world of difference. Taking the time to say a word or phrase just so can do the job of a hundred words or more unmindfully spoken. Patient preaching knows to notice the punctuation marks of a sermon, and the spaces between the words. Patient preaching not only speaks to be heard, but speaks to be felt. Patient preaching is not afraid to hold tension in a sermon—and doubt, and fear, and silence. The spaces provide a place for tears, and engagement with our deeper selves and God. The spaces of patient preaching also make sufficient room for faith and grace.

By the way, just so you know, at the time of this writing, Jimmy Scott is still singing at seventy-eight years of age.

## A Blues Sermon

Livey Bennett was one of my son's best friends. He spent the night at our home often. He did so on one April evening in 2003. The next night he was shot and killed in an altercation after a dance at a church hall. Livey's death broke many hearts, including my son's and my own. Livey's mother asked if I would conduct his funeral and preach his eulogy.

### *Livey's Gifts*
### *1 Corinthians 12:4*

I

When the call came early last Saturday morning and I first heard the heart-wrenching news, my first response was anger.

How could such a thing have happened?

How could such bright light be put out just like that?

How could Livey be snatched away so suddenly?

When we feel violated and wronged, it is only natural and human to be angry. The Christian faith does not teach us that we should or can live without ever getting angry. Ephesians 4:26 does warn against letting "the sun go down on [our] anger." We should not, we cannot, stay angry. If we stay angry, we run the risk of becoming our anger. If we become our anger, then we add to the spirit of angry violence that took Livey from us. If anger must have a hold on us for a moment, we cannot let it have us.

*Livey deserves more than our anger about his death. He deserves better than that. Our world deserves better than that.*

Sometimes grieving involves anger; all the time, grieving involves pain. But if we are to experience love, pain cannot be avoided. Pain is a price we pay for loving. If we didn't love so, we wouldn't hurt so. If we didn't care about Livey, his death wouldn't hurt us so.

*It is because we care and we love that we hurt.*

What do we do with our grief, with our anger, with our pain? We can lean on each other. And, we can lean on God. First Peter 5:7 says we don't have to carry the hurt by ourselves: *Place your cares (your pains and hurts) with God, because God cares for you.*

Slowly, through the anger, through our common grief and pain, about Livey's death we can move to a place of gratitude and joy for Livey's life. And there's much to celebrate about his short but full life. In 1 Corinthians 12:4-6, these words are found: "Now there are varieties of gifts, but the same Spirit; and there are varieties of services, but the same Lord; and there are varieties of activities, but it is the same God who activates all of them in everyone."

Thank God for Livey's gifts!

## II

Livey had an extraordinary gift for being alive. He had a vibrant, lively spirit.

Take away the *y* from his name and you are left with L-I-V-E. Livey lived. Livey was alive with great passion and energy enough for five or six people. I think about the introduction of that famous Saturday night television show: "Live from New York, it's *Saturday Night Live*!" "Live from Randolph, it's Livey Bennett Live!" He was so full of fun and laughter and volume. You knew when Livey was in the house.

And for someone who didn't drive, Livey was everywhere! He walked, took the bus, got rides, and he had a scooter for a while.

Livey was everywhere:

Randolph High

Burger King

McDonald's

Sudbury Farms Food Store

There was no telling when or where Livey would turn up. I was exercising one morning, and suddenly, out of nowhere, his face appeared at my window. "Mr. Jones, open the door!"

And the gift within the gift of his aliveness was that it was about being who he was. Livey enjoyed being Livey! So he wore his football jersey backwards.

We are only truly alive when we are truly ourselves.

III

Livey had the gift of a radically friendly spirit, which he shared with everyone. What a procession of honor last night in tribute to his friendly spirit that touched so many, so many different kinds of people.

His friendly spirit crossed racial lines,

crossed age lines,

crossed gender lines,

crossed class lines,

in-crowd/out-crowd lines,

popular/not-so-popular lines.

We should not blind ourselves to the challenge before us. Livey challenges us, each of us, to face our fears, to take more risks with friendships, to work harder at developing bonds of friendships with people who are different. Difference does not mean deficient. And as Martin Luther King, Jr., said, "We are all tied together in a single garment of destiny."

## IV

Thank God for Livey's liveliness, his friendliness, and his tenderness. Yes, Livey loved football, and yes he was loud, but Livey had a soft side. I overheard someone say last night at the wake, "Livey had a good heart." His uncle told me that at church services he'd take Livey to, on more than one occasion he saw a tear trickle down Livey's cheek. Right here at First Baptist there is a children's moment during each worship service. Children ages five to eleven come forward, and sixteen-year-old Livey, sitting and listening with the children.

He loved his family; he adored his mother, who adored him. So what if he ate half the chocolates he gave her this past Valentine's Day. She still has the beautiful pendant of a dozen roses that he also gave her to cherish forever his memory and his spirit, which lives on.

V

I end our eulogy to Livey with words that came to me as I sat with my grief one morning this week. I thought about Livey and wept. And I thought about where he is now, and I found myself writing this:

## Look Out Heaven!

*Look out heaven*
*That's Livey Bennett*

*He's full of big fun and*
*He's filled with loud laughter*

*Look out heaven*
*That's Livey Bennett*

*He's the one on the scooter rolling, roaring down*
*heaven's great boulevards and small side streets*

*He's the one talking to everyone in heaven's grocery store*

*He's the one with his robe on backwards*
*and his halo tilted to the side*

*Look out heaven*
*That's Livey Bennett*

*It won't be long before all of you will know him,*
*and notice*
*that things are even more lively*
*up in glory.*

## Exercises and Resources

1. What made you sad as a child?
2. How did you deal with your pain as a child?
3. What saddens you now?
4. How do you address your sadness as an adult?
5. Listen to Billie Holiday (*The Essential Billie Holiday*), John Coltrane (*A Love Supreme*), and/or Jimmy Scott (*The Savoy Years and More*, and *But Beautiful*). Where does their music take you? What does it say to you? How might their song styling inform your preaching?
6. How do you tend to address pain and suffering in your preaching?
7. Remain in touch with your own suffering through journaling, sharing with your spouse, talking with friends, and/or conversing with a spiritual director.
8. Live your life at a sacred, savoring pace. For more information visit www.savoringpace.com.

NOTES

1. Cone, *The Spirituals and the Blues*, 116-18.
2. Album notes, *Lady Day: The Complete Billie Holiday on Columbia, 1933–1944* (Columbia Records, 2001).
3. Ibid.
4. Ibid.
5. As quoted in Ashley Kahn, *A Love Supreme: The Story of John Coltrane's Signature Album* (New York: Viking, 2002), xxii.
6. From Paul D. Zimmerman (with Ruth Ross), "The New Jazz," *Newsweek* (December 12, 1966), 108; and Paul D. Zimmerman, "Death of a Jazzman," *Newsweek* (July 31, 1967), 78-79. As quoted in Lewis Porter, *John Coltrane: His Life and Music* (Ann Arbor: The University of Michigan Press,1998), 232.
7. David Ritz, *Faith in Time: The Life of Jimmy Scott* (Cambridge, MA: Da Capo Press, 2002), xv.
8. Ibid., xiv.
9. Ibid., xiv-xv.

CHAPTER EIGHT

# The Swing of Preaching

*The gloom of the world is but a shadow. Behind it, yet within our reach, is joy. Take joy!*

—Fra Giovanni

*If God let you sprout wings you oughta have sense enough not to let nobody make you wear something that gits in the way of flyin'.*

—Ralph Ellison, *Flying Home*

*If I can't dance, I don't want to be part of your revolution.*

—Emma Goldman, community activist

When jazz is truly swinging, the universe is hard-pressed to present a greater manifestation of joy.

Jazz was never more joyful than on July 8, 1956, at the Newport Jazz Festival in Newport, Rhode Island. It was around midnight when Duke Ellington and his band of fifteen persons took the stage for their second set. After several selections, the maestro introduced "Diminuendo in Blue" and "Crescendo in Blue," which Ellington had written in 1938, but the band had not performed them much in recent years. In fact, Paul Gonsalves, the tenor saxophonist tapped to solo in the middle of the song, didn't even know the piece. Ellington reassured him, telling him that he would guide him in and out of the solo. "Just get out there and blow your tail off," Ellington said. "You've done it before." What happened next took Newport and the entire jazz world by joyous storm. Jana Tull Steed tells the story:

> Duke opened "Diminuendo and Crescendo" with four rhythmic choruses. Duke was punctuating his piano playing with gutteral [sic] murmurs and shouted exclamations. Out of the crowd's sight, Count Basie's drummer Jo Jones egged on the rhythm section by slapping a rolled-up newspaper against the stage. The band answered, Duke came back for two more choruses to set up Gonsalves. Paul took over, always in sync with the driving rhythm behind him. At about the seventh chorus, the crowd began to catch fire.... A platinum blonde in a black dress began dancing in one of the box seats, recalled one witness. Couples broke into jitterbug, and soon all seven thousand fans were on their feet, dancing, cheering, clapping—but still listening to the phenomenal performance. The band and the crowd were one now and Gonsalves kept going and did not stop until he had played twenty-seven choruses of "blazing hot jazz." The baton was passed onto the band, and by the time William "Cat" Anderson's trumpet was in the stratosphere, they had played an unprecedented fifty-nine choruses. The producer and the police were worried about a riot and tried to get Ellington to stop right there. Duke wagged his finger at them, then shook his head and proceeded to

> cool down the crowd the same way he heated it up—with more music.[1]

You can hear this performance on *Ellington at Newport 1956* (20-bit digitally remastered; Sony, 1999). The recording was re-released just as I was preparing to teach the first Jazz of Preaching class at Andover Newton Theological School—just in time.

Another favorite joy snapshot of jazz is a picture of pianist Thelonious Monk dancing. Known for his unorthodox manner and musical style, Monk would literally get up in the middle of a performance and dance. Former band member Ben Riley remembers:

> When his music was happening, then he'd get up and do his little dance. 'Cause he was feeling good, and he knew where you were and the music was swinging, and that's what he wanted. So, he said, "Well, I don't have to play now. You're making it happen."
>
> I felt that him dancing meant that the music was happening. 'Cause he used say, "I want you to swing hard, swing very hard, and then swing as hard as you can swing." See? So, every time he danced, man, that just meant that something was happening with us and that we needed to just give it some more energy, some more energy.[2]

When I think of jazz and joy, I think of Ellington and his band that night, I think of Monk, and I think of Ella Fitzgerald and Louis Armstrong. Perhaps the two greatest jazz souls of all, Fitzgerald and Armstrong produced one of the most delightful albums you'll ever hear. *The Complete Ella Fitzgerald and Louis Armstrong* (Polygram Records, 1997) contains my favorite jazz selection, "You Can't Take That Away from Me." The two are magnificent. They are singing and playing together at the height of their musical powers, and enjoying every second of it. The picture on the cover says it all. Ella is lost in a trance of a smile, and Louie is in mid-laughter. What an album; what a picture; what a legacy of joy! Even when diseases were having their way with the bodies of these jazz giants, Fitzgerald and Armstrong's joy reigned supreme. The final scene of Ken Burns's *Jazz* has Armstrong taking to the stage in a final triumphant rendition of "Sleepy Time Down South." His smile that night was brighter than the stars. Through various serious illnesses Ella Fitzgerald continued to manifest a vocal dexterity and levity of spirit that was, as far as I was concerned, substantive proof for the existence of God.

## Joy and Preaching

When it comes to joy in preaching, I think Ella Fitzgerald and Louie Armstrong hold the key. They were able to bring joy to their music because they experienced joy in their living. Joyful preaching is found less in technique and more in our daring to become joyful human beings. If we would be joyful preachers, we would first be people of joy.

Becoming persons of joy means giving ourselves permission to be happy. This can seem insensitive and selfish in a world filled with so much grief. Yet the power to address and endure suffering is directly related to our capacity to sing in the storm. Joy is the great revolutionary act. It keeps us going against all odds. The great theme of our faith—Resurrection—is reason for Newport-jazz-joy, and then some. Resurrection incites laughing aloud because God and good are never dead and done.

Children don't apologize for being joyful. As children, we gravitate toward joy even when circumstances dictate sadness. Recently, I marveled at a picture of three young surviving siblings of a tragic airplane crash. Both parents and two children died in the crash. The three brothers who lived were injured, one so severely that his left leg had to be amputated below the knee. The picture shows the brothers, only six weeks removed from the accident and now living with relatives, in the backyard of their new home. Two of the boys are smiling; one, the youngest is laughing, not apart from his pain, I presume, but through it.

These brothers and our brother Jesus, who lived, died, and lived, signal to us that we can, in time, grab our joy back after it has been snatched away by suffering. Though not an easy reaching, it is a necessary one if we are to journey on through our sweet-bitter-sweet world in sacrifice and delight. Joy in preaching is less a matter of cultivating techniques and more a matter of claiming gifts.

## Claiming Personhood and Love

In 1784 Sir Henry Raeburn, one of Scotland's most popular painters, painted *The Reverend Robert Walker Skating on Duddingston Loch.* In the picture, a church minister is ice-skating, very properly and rigidly, but ice-skating nonetheless. In addition to his manner, the minister's clothing is indicative of his "reverendness." His conservative black suit, stockings, and hat are a dead giveaway. One of the messages I receive from the painting is that even while engaging in a recreational activity, this man was undoubtedly "the Reverend" Robert Walker.

If we are not careful, we can allow who we are to be completely overtaken by roles and expectations that, while helping to make us who we are, should never define us completely. As I gazed at the picture, I wondered if there were ever times when "the Reverend Robert Walker" was simply "Robert Walker." Did he have a sense of his own holy and unique personhood apart from the black suit and apart from his role as a minister? Was he capable of celebrating life not just as a member of the clergy, but also as a child and as a child of God?

While self-sacrifice is an essential part of ministry, self-destruction is not. In fact, when you push aside your authentic humanness in pursuit of serving God, you end up losing some of God's "best stuff" for ministry: your unique constellation of traits, habits, preferences, quirks, and everything else that makes you you.

Allowing more time in your weekly schedule for doing things you enjoy away from ministry, and celebrating a prayer and play day each week are ways to preserve selfhood. Another way to affirm personhood is noticing yourself more as part of your daily devotion. Don't worry; God won't mind. God is more concerned about our not noticing. This practice will remind you of yourself before the credentials and the accomplishments, and keep before you the self that God sees first when God sees you.

Each day, in ways that are most comfortable and meaningful for you, thank God for the you that you are, and for God's loving acceptance of you as you are. Accept your acceptance. Relaxing in God's loving embrace, our ministries are less likely to deteriorate into endless pursuits for acceptance and worth. We are no longer in search of what we already have. Attending to sacred selfhood unleashes a powerful stream of love and grace, the vital source of meaningful and joyful preaching and ministry.

# A Swing Sermon/Address

## *"Ministers Who Sing and Tremble" (Andover Newton Theological School Commencement Address, Spring 2001)*

I

First, let me extend heartfelt gratitude to you for bestowing on me this tremendous honor. Second, and I think I speak for full-time and adjunct faculty on this, thank you for being our teachers as well as our students.

While flying home from Pittsburgh a week ago, I began reading Mary Oliver's book-length, seven-part poem about questioning and discovering, *The Leaf and the Cloud*. I did not get very far. Phrases and images kept stopping me. You can expect that sort of thing from a poet who says, as does Oliver, "I am a woman of sixty years old, and glory is my work."[3] After taking forty minutes to read part 1 (a mammoth six and a quarter pages), I set my sights on part 2. I had achieved a steady, savoring reading pace when I found myself stalled again. Oliver writes of thick and heavy grass in summer, adding

> Sparrows swing on them, they bend down.
> When the sparrow sings, its whole body trembles.[4]

"When the sparrow sings, its whole body trembles."

Thirty thousand feet above ground, I became entranced with the singing, trembling sparrow. Minutes later, I found myself praying an unexpected prayer for you. I began praying for you to be ministers who sing and tremble.

II

As you minister, you must sing. Now that doesn't necessarily mean that [musically gifted graduating seniors] have an unfair advantage in ministry. I mean for you to sing, broadly interpreted; and my precise point is that you not simply talk your way through ministry. I do not mean to denigrate talk, that would have severe vocational repercussions.

It has been said that words are a kind of action, and action a kind of word. Mark Twain once said that the difference between the right word and the wrong word is the difference between lightning and a lightning bug. Marlo Thomas has edited a new book entitled *The Right Words at the Right Time* (Atria Books, 2002). It's an interesting collection of testimonies from well-known people about the words that have had the most significant impact on their lives.

Thank God for words!

Thank God for telling!

When we were growing up in the bayou land of Louisiana, my brothers and I had a song we would lead the youth choir in singing at the Mount Hermon Baptist Church: "I said I wasn't gonna tell nobody but I couldn't keep it to myself." The song celebrates the reality of "testifying," telling people about God's goodness.

We celebrate words and telling!

All of you are "tellers," people of the word. And in a few moments you will have a degree to prove it. You will have substantially raised the bar of expectation regarding your ability to use words to tell the story.

But beware!

In her wonderful, small book *When God Is Silent*, Barbara Brown Taylor criticizes our having made Christianity an overly talkative religion. This is why I wish for you not just a talking, but a singing, ministry. Even the clearest, truest, and most beautiful spoken words fall short when it comes to sharing the gospel.

So we must sing, in all the ways that we can

Sing:

From the depths of your soul

dream and dance,

imagine and create,

laugh, leap, and

sometimes limp.

Don't forget to be still,

because there is no singing, no music

without silence.

Some of the most important words I've read are these from one Abraham Joshua Heschel:

> The strength of faith is in silence, and in words that hibernate and wait. Uttered faith must come out as surplus of silence, as the fruit of lived faith, of enduring intimacy.

Saying, talking, no matter how eloquent and passionate, is not enough. I have never forgotten the title of a preaching book I read some years back: *I've Got the Word in Me, and I Can Sing It You Know*. You must sing It; it is impossible to just say It.[5]

## III

"When the sparrow sings, its whole body trembles."

Trembles.

I wondered whether or not Oliver meant all sparrows tremble or just the one she may have been observing at the time. I did some investigating. I spoke with a member of the graduating class who is an avid bird watcher. I spoke with a bird store owner in Orleans, Massachusetts. The bird watchers I spoke with did not completely refute or verify Oliver's claim about all or some sparrows trembling all over when they sing.

What difference? I am sure that I want you to tremble. And I know why. I want you to tremble from daring to hold and honor tension. Faithful ministry resists easy retreats from tension.

Patience and restraint will be important to your ministries, but so will candor and agitation—tension breeders for sure.

How can entrenched evil and complicit denial be unearthed apart from tension, grief, and, yes, suffering? Where there would be healing, often, if not always, there must first be confrontation. Remember Martin Luther King's words in "Letter from Birmingham Jail." Writing to clergy who trembled for the wrong reason, fearfulness in the face of social change, King said; "I have earnestly opposed violent tension, but there is a type of constructive, nonviolent tension which is necessary for growth."

Honoring and holding tension will have you trembling, I hope. And I pray that you tremble for another reason: tremble with quivering astonishment and aroused awe before the story.

May the pathos of the story cause you to tremble.

Were you there when they crucified my Lord?
Were you there when they crucified my Lord?

Oh sometimes it causes me to tremble, tremble, tremble.
Were you there when they crucified my Lord?

And may the *promise* of the story evoke the excited shaking of hope.

[We] are bound for the promised land;
[We] are bound for the promised land.
O who will come and go with me?
[We] are bound for the promised land.

## IV

*Ministers who sing and tremble, always?*

No, not always. There will be those times when you will not feel like singing, and the trembling will give way to numbness. Don't worry.

In a recent article the great jazz/blues singer Cassandra Wilson (you knew the jazz was coming, didn't you?) says,

> By the end of 1999, I was exhausted. I had done four albums since 1993, each followed by a long tour and one led right into the next. So I needed to take some time off, and I went home to get my bearings. I always go home when I want to gather the information I need to move forward.[6]

When you lose your song and your tremble, go home.

Go home.

Remember that you are God's child.

Go home.

Abide under the waterfall of God's love.

Go home.

Accept your holy acceptance.

Go home.

Know afresh and anew that you are the beloved of God, and that, in the words of Emilie Townes,

> we are not dipped
> we are not sprinkled
> we are not immersed
> we are washed in the grace of God.[7]

## Exercises and Resources

1. What brought you joy as a child?
2. What makes you laugh now?
3. What are some of your favorite joy places in Scripture?
4. How do you cultivate your leisure life?
5. Listen to *Ellington at Newport*, and anything at all by Ella Fitzgerald and Louis Armstrong. How might this music inform your preaching?
6. Master the arts of storytelling and joke-telling. A good resource is *Improving Your Storytelling*, by Doug Lipman (August House Publications, 1999).
7. Read and study *Celebration and Experience in Preaching*, by Henry Mitchell (Abingdon Press, 1990), and *They Like to Never Quit Praising God*, by Frank A. Thomas (United Church Press, 1997).
8. Receive God's love afresh and anew every day. Imagine various ways of doing so. For example, you may want to swim in the waters of God's love. Use the power of

imagination to accept your acceptance each day. That's where the joy is.

## Notes

1. Steed, *Duke Ellington: A Spiritual Biography*, 102.

2. Quincy Troupe and Ben Riley, "Remembering Thelonious Monk: When the Music Was Happening Then He'd Get Up and Do His Little Dance," in *The Jazz Cadence of American Culture*, edited by Robert G. O'Meally (New York: Columbia University Press, 1998), 106.

3. Mary Oliver, *The Leaf and the Cloud: A Poem* (New York: DaCapo Press, 2001), 10.

4. Oliver, *The Leaf and the Cloud*, 10.

5. *Moral Grandeur*, 264.

6. Geoffrey Himes, "The New Standard," *JazzTimes* (May 2002), 55.

7. Emilie Townes, *In a Blaze of Glory* (Nashville: Abingdon Press, 1995), 47.